MW01388120

Jerry O. Waters: Born To Be A Coach

Author
Rev. Odell Cleveland

Cover by Courtney M. Chavis, Greensboro, NC

Cover Photographs USC Upstate Athletics
Department

ISBN -13: 978-0615732190
ISBN-10: 0615732194

Preface

This book started after Coach Jerry Waters learned of my book ***Pracademics and Community Change (Cleveland and Wineburg Lyceum Book, Inc. 2011).*** He said that he has been thinking about writing a book for years and asked would I help him. I said, "Coach I would be honored to help you write your book." I personally know of a number of people who had received many benefits from their association with Coach Jerry Waters. I wanted to introduce him to the world, by collecting and preserving reminiscences of his accomplishments, and pass on his philosophy to those who may not have known him, but could possibly benefit from being introduced to him through this work.

To facilitate the work, a former high school (Middleton High School – 1976-78) and college (University of South Carolina Spartanburg – 1981-1983) basketball player of Coach Waters, used Facebook, Emails, YouTube, Twitter and phone calls to contact many who knew him. I requested that they communicate directly with me. Without their cooperation, confidence and suggestions the task would have been very difficult.   I travelled many miles to interview Coach Waters, former players, coaches, students, family, and friends.

I delved into and analyzed boxes of memorabilia to find the core principles of Coach Jerry Waters' success.

Dedication

This book is dedicated to Jeffrey and Jason Waters, my sons.

Both of my sons grew up in an atmosphere of sports. With me being a coach, both Jeff and Jason were always around sports, and I spent a lot of time encouraging them to participate in things that interested them. They learned early, the importance of being a part of a team. Jeff and Jason played baseball and basketball in their early years, and both gravitated towards basketball as their sport in high school. Jeff and Jason were very good high school players at Boiling Springs High School in Spartanburg, SC.

At the completion of Jeff's senior year he received a grant-in-aid to play basketball at the University of South Carolina Spartanburg. I just happened to be the coach at USCS during his college career. Jeff was a point guard on a team that averaged 28 wins per season and had 4 years of winning district championships and going on to post-season play. Jason had always wanted to attend the University of Georgia. He earned an academic scholarship to UGA and also worked as a student assistant for the basketball team all four years.

He spent a fifth year at UGA and received a master's degree while continuing to work as a graduate assistant with the basketball team. During Jason's last two years at UGA, I was an assistant coach for the Bulldogs. It was an incredible experience for me to be with both of them during these years. What a real blessing for a father to share in all those wonderful experiences!

It gives me great pleasure to dedicate this book, *Born to be a Coach*, to my two sons. Thanks for your dedication. Even though I was your coach, you taught me more than you will ever comprehend. Thank you for being on my team. I love you! Jason and Jeff still have a close relationship. They now have sons of their own to teach. Jason is an attorney and Jeff is an insurance agent.

Jerry O. Waters

Acknowledgments

I am grateful to the following people, for their help with the writing of this book:

Bob and Dottie Anderson
Ted and Charles Conrad
Sandra Waters Cobb
Coach Wayne Dobbs
Bill Drake
Bill English
Ron Garner
Mike Hall
John D. and Georgeanna Marlow Kicklighter
Lonie Kicklighter
Gary Leonard
Jim Littlefield
Stephanie Mathis
Elizabeth (Susie) Kicklighter McMullan
Tom Moses
Eddie and Ann Payne
Billy Port
Senator Glenn G. Reese
Andy Solomon
Pete and Joe Smyth

****
Cal Tee Solutions, LLC -- pictures
Chapman High School -- pictures

DLW Entertainment, Inc. -- pictures
Glennville High School Yearbook -- pictures
Middleton High School Yearbook -- pictures
Pinewood Christian Academy -- pictures
University of Georgia Athletics -- pictures
U SC Upstate Athletics Department -- pictures

Introduction

It was my intention to use the results of this research simply as a documentary of Coach Jerry Waters' Life. But when I informed him- just how much he and his philosophy had influenced the lives of so many people and when he learned of the accomplishments many of these people, he wondered if there was a common factor in their lives that could be attributed to his work with them.

I concluded that it would be important to know how Jerry Waters became Coach Jerry O. Waters. What was it in his life that sets him above the ordinary? Was it his work ethics? Was it his intelligence? Did his environment have a bearing on his success? Or was he simply blessed to have stumbled upon extraordinarily talented players? Coach Waters' childhood is dealt with only to note how it affected his circumstance, and in tracing the development of his mind.

One cannot tell Coach Waters' life story without including a few of his legendary basketball defensive plays like the *90 Z, 50 Z or HALF-COURT TRAP.* A huge part of his life centered on the development of strategic plays and player developments that led to seven high school state championships, four in South Carolina and three in Georgia. Coach Waters Crown Jewel was the 1982 NAIA National Championship. Basketball was his life and I will depict its basketball core here.

In some chapters I will be writing about my personal experiences. In other chapters I will simply use the powerful words from other players and coaches who worked with Coach Waters during his basketball heyday. But it is Waters the man, as seen by his players and revealed by his words and deeds that I have tried to capture. This is a book of truth blended with a subtle irony? But that analysis is for you the reader to decide.

Table of Contents
Preface
Dedication
Acknowledgments
Introduction

Chapters

Chapter 1 - *The St. Andrews High/ Middleton High
School Years*

Chapter 2 - *Jerry the College Coach and Recruiter*

Chapter 3 - *Coach Waters leaves USCS for the
University of Georgia*

Chapter 4 - *Coach Waters returns home to coach
Pinewood Christian Academy*

Chapter 5 - *Chapman High School, Inman, SC*

Chapter 6 - *Next Play --- Coach Waters draws up
the "next play" for his life*

Appendix 1… *X's and O's, 50Z and 90Z Press
Defense*

Appendix 2… *SPIN Offense*

Appendix 3… *Photo Section*

Chapter 1 --- The St. Andrews High/Middleton High School Years

Mention the name Jerry O. Waters, to those who knew him in the late 1960's while he coached at St. Andrews High School, you will hear, "Jerry was old school, hard core." "He was your coach, not your friend." He was so hardcore that he sometimes came across as "not being very nice." All he cared about was winning, whether it was coaching baseball, football or basketball; the young coach was only focused on one thing, winning. You see, that's the only way Jerry Waters knew how to approach athletics. He was a five-sport letterman during his senior year in 1962, playing varsity football, basketball, track, tennis and baseball for the Bulldogs of Glennville High, Glennville, Georgia.

Life for young Jerry wasn't always easy. He grew up in a small southern town in a family who emphasized working hard for what you wanted in life. He started playing sports at an early age with the older and bigger boys in the neighborhood, many of whom were his cousins, who would rough him up, "toughen" him up.

Those early lessons learned from the toughness

of competition became central to Jerry's views of life. John D. Kicklighter, his older cousin, who lived next door, was one of his influential "toughness" teachers early on. John's father, Mr. Fess Kicklighter was Coach Waters' great uncle on his maternal grandmother's side.

Coach Waters and his sister, Sandra Waters Cobb spent most of their early years with his grandmother Ms. Lonie Kicklighter, while his father and mother worked at the local Red & White Food Store, better known by the locals as Burns Food Palace. His father was the produce manager and his mother was a cashier. For years, young Jerry would work after school as a bag boy at Burns food. Years later, his father became a furniture salesman for Danner Furniture.

Jerry's grandmother lived across the street from the local baseball field. As a young boy, Jerry was allowed to be   the ball boy or batboy during most of the home games. He enjoyed the encouragement he received from the coaches. As he continued to get older, Jerry played sports year round. He soon gained the reputation of being a pretty good athletic, a self-described "sports fanatic." He learned so much more than sports from his coaches; he learned life's lessons. He loved it!

Coach Waters knew in the seventh grade that he wanted to be a coach for the rest of his life. After graduation from high school, Waters received a baseball scholarship to attend Georgia Southern University. The situation at Georgia Southern didn't work out and Coach Waters soon found himself back home in Glennville, working a construction job. He remembers the toll that the hard work was taking on his body and the encouraging words that his grandmother Lonie always shared with him.

About a year later he received a call from Coach Wayne Dobbs, baseball coach at Brewton Parker Junior College located in Mount Vernon, Georgia.

Coach Dobbs wanted to know, if he wanted to play baseball there. Waters leaped at the opportunity for a second chance at college.

While at Brewton Parker, Jerry helped out Coach Dobbs with the basketball team during basketball season and starting to like basketball even more than baseball. Two years later, Coach Dobbs got a job as the head baseball coach at Belmont University and recruited Waters to play at Belmont.

Years later, Coach Waters reflected on his experiences at Belmont, he states that he was 14 hours away from home and he only knew the coaches and the players. However, once a month he would receive a package in the mail from his grandmother, Ms. Lonie Kicklighter. The package would consist of homemade peanut butter cookies, five dollars, and hand written letter full of words of encouragement that always ended with "remember, why you are there."

Jerry was very close to his grandmother and she always believed in him. He would never want to disappoint her. He knew that she was making a personal sacrifice by sending his monthly care packages. Jerry and Lonie's ties were so strong, a grandmother's love. Lonie Kicklighter wanted nothing more than to see her grandson Jerry, succeed in life. Jerry Waters wanted nothing more than to please Lonie. Tears still run down his face as he reflects on the relationship that he once shared with his grandmother.

During this time period, another Kicklighter would be following Waters' progress. His cousin John D. Kicklighter also encouraged him to stay focused on his studies, and told him that after graduation he would help Jerry find a job.

John D. Kicklighter was Coach Waters' cousin and mentor, originally coached boys' basketball at St. Andrews High School "Rocks" and his 1967-68 team won the state championship. Coach Waters was his assistant that year. St. Andrews High School was known throughout the state for its academic achievements and was the "flagship" high school in district 10, Charleston, SC.

Superintendent C.E. Williams viewed St. Andrews as the beautiful feather in his hat. St. Andrews was the predominately white school, while Wallace High School was the predominately black. Facing the pressure of integration, in 1968, the district responded by allowing C. E. Williams Junior High to house ninth and tenth grade students. And in 1969 through 1970, the district instituted a practice referred to as "Freedom of Choice," which allowed the black students, mainly from Wallace High, to choose between attending St. Andrews and staying at Wallace. Eventually Wallace was no longer a high school.

In 1971, Middleton High was founded and John D. Kicklighter was selected as the principal to lead this newly formed school in the mist of segregation.

Rufus German, from Wallace High joined Kicklighter as his assistant principal, to help form a dynamic leadership team along with so many other committed teachers, administrators and staff. Some of the teachers left C.E. Williams Junior High to join the teaching ranks of the newly formed Middleton High School.

Many of the people interviewed for this book either attended, taught, or worked at St. Andrews, Wallace, C. E. Williams, and/or Middleton High, and had firsthand experiences, as it was "Coach Waters 'world" during those turbulent years. Many remember the year when the two schools combined their football team and named it the "RazorRocks." Much was mentioned about the "grown-ups" making important decisions after the high school games at Gene's Haufbrau's bar, a popular hangout for some teachers, administrators, coaches, and referees.

When one thinks about the early Middleton High school years, it's very easy to focus only on the great basketball teams. In 1970, Coach Jerry O. Waters accepted the Head Basketball job at the newly opened Middleton High. The consensus of interviewees speculated that Coach Waters decided to leave St. Andrews and accept the Middleton job was because he and John Kicklighter were well aware of the *school district lines* as they were being drawn, and both men had a very good idea of where all of the good athletes lived.

Many interviewees said that two young basketball players Chris White, and William "Billy" Graham, were the "reasons" he took the job. Yes, Jerry O. Waters was born and raised in a small southern town, but Jerry knew talented players when he saw them. Coach Jerry O. Waters was smart, especially so, when it came to understanding basketball talent. YES, Chris White and William "Billy" Graham were that good!

Over the next eight years, Coach Waters' teams won 226 games and lost only 36. Middleton won six Conference Titles, three State Championships and finished State Runner –Up twice. The Razorbacks won 55 games in a row, 68 consecutive conference games, and were unbeaten at home for over three years. However, reflecting back to the late 60's and the early 70's and the country's struggle with Civil Rights, race, and school segregation, it is hard to imagine a new high school succeeding in any arena, academic and/or athletics in such a changing and delicate social environment.

Records document that the school was closed twice because of "mysterious fires." The first fire occurred in 1970. It damaged the main office entrance and the library that was located above the office. The second fire occurred in 1972, the very day that the team was playing in the lower state tournament. I once had the good fortune of meeting John Kicklighter at a Celebrity Awards Banquet and we exchanged pleasantries. However, I really did not fully understand the role that he played at Middleton until I sat down at Melvin's Bar-B-Que located in Mount Pleasant, South Carolina and interviewed his daughter Elizabeth Susie Kicklighter McMullan for hours. Without her frankness about her dad, my job would have been tougher. She shared with me a story about her dad, Middleton's legendary leader and principal. John D. Kicklighter was known to spend many nights walking the halls and occasionally spending the night in the school to make sure that no one would burn his school down.

You see, John D. Kicklighter was the quiet leader who was the heart and soul of the young Middleton High School. Rumors have it that he came up with the idea of the mascot as the Razorbacks from an old army buddy who was from Arkansas and always talked about the University of Arkansas, Razorbacks.

In the beginning, when St. Andrews and Middleton competed in a high school athletic contest, you could always hear the St. Andrews' cheerleaders and students shouting "Beat the junior high, beat the junior high!" Middleton High celebrated *Razorback Day* as their independence day, the day they were no longer a part of St. Andrews High. St. Andrews immediately became Middleton's archrival, and even though both schools no longer exist, many alumni still see each other as rivals.

Surprisingly, the main interviews about those early years came from two former teachers - Pete Smyth and Gary Leonard. I was touched to hear Pete's voice change and see the tears well-up in his eyes as we sat at the table in the Earth Fare on Folly Road Boulevard. During a separate interview with Gary Leonard, while sitting at a table at the Sesame Burgers and Beer restaurant located in the Citadel Mall, his voice trembled also as the reflected back on the years between 1972 and 1979. He looked me straight in my eyes and referred to those years at Middleton as "Camelot."

When I questioned both men about the word

"Camelot", they both referred to the "feeling" that many had at Middleton. It was a "new idea" for whites and blacks to go to school together. Additionally, the prevailing attitude was "us (Middleton) against the world." Middleton High School's varsity basketball program was the single thing that galvanized the whole school. However, when it came to school pride and notoriety, the wonderful "Middleton Singers" directed by Page Gregory Kelly, should not be left out of what also brought the school together.

As a teenager, growing up playing basketball on the asphalt courts of our neighborhood park, nestled in the all black community of Ashleyville, a subdivision of Charleston, South Carolina, which the locals referred to as "West of the Ashley," I learned to play organized basketball at the St. Andrews Park and Recreation gym located on playground road. While in the 7th grade at C. E. Williams Middle School, I was a part of the St. Andrews High School Junior Varsity basketball team and the following year I was a part of the Middleton High School junior varsity basketball team. That's when I first heard of the legendary Coach Jerry Waters.

As a ninth grader, I tried out for the varsity basketball team and made it. After a few days of practice, I decided that I really didn't like Coach Waters. I was bothered by the way Coach would yell at other players. I thought that he was too tough. At that time, I had not yet had a personal run-in with Coach during practice. However, I knew that my number would come up.

Everybody's number would eventually come up with Coach. As a 17 year old freshman with a "racial chip" on my shoulders, I had no tolerance for an old white guy jumping in my face and yelling and screaming at me for any little mistake or lack of effort in practice. You see, I always felt that for Jerry, it was not always about the mistakes, and/or lack of effort. I believed that Coach used these opportunities to exercise control over people, in the tone of "I will break you down mentally and I will build you back up as the player that I want you to be. "

That approach just didn't sit well with me. I just would not allow Jerry Waters or any other coach to have that kind of mental control over me. My mothers, Mrs. Glenda Adams Cleveland along with my grandfather Tecumseh Earnest Adams, were the only two people who possessed that kind of influence and control over me.

Even though I really didn't care for Coach during practice, I always believed he wanted to push his players to their individual breaking points. I liked the mental wars that he and I had during practices. You see, I was known as "not a practice player," meaning that I did not always come to practice on time, or even come at all. If something more important came up, like riding home on another school bus to continue a conversation with a young woman that I was interested in dating, there simply was no basketball practice that day.

The truth is, I did not always take Middleton basketball as serious as Coach Waters did. On one occasion, after I did not show up to practice at all, I saw Jerry's old station wagon parked in front of my house. I waited around the corner until he left; I then walked in the door to greet my mother, to soon learn that Coach told my mother about me skipping practice. My mother called my grandfather. I knew immediately that I was in big trouble, especially after they both finished talking to me about accountability, commitment, and the team depending on me.

That was the end of skipping practice, or being late for practice again. In my mind then, Coach "ratted me out, to get me straight" to the two people whom I loved and respected the most.

To Coach Waters' credit, he was a master, and still is to this day, at understanding his player's family structure and knowing who held the influence in the family. I remember telling my teammates the next day in school that coach "ratted" me out and I got in trouble with Papa T. They all knew he was my grandfather and what I was saying in between the lines.

So, there I was at 17 years old, with a racial chip on my shoulder, stuck between a rock and a hard place. I was mad at Jerry for ratting on me, but never *ever* wanting to disappoint my mother and grandfather again. So, I decided that I would never miss practice again, but that I still was not going to let Coach break me. I avoided Coach all day in school and was one of the first players in the locker room to get dressed for practice. I knew that I would have to do something crazy like publically apologizing to my teammates for missing practice, and run what Jerry fondly referred to a suicides.

Suicides drills consisted of a player(s) standing at the end of the basketball court at the baseline. There was Coach Waters holding a stopwatch in his hand, and later he used a game clock to time us. Once Coach said "go," the player had to race to the first foul line, touch the line, and then race back to the baseline, touch it, then run from the baseline and touch the half court line, race back and touch the original baseline, race from the baseline to the foul line at the other end of the court, touch that line, then race back to the original baseline, and touch it. Then the player would have to race from the original baseline to the baseline on the other end of the court and touch the line and then race back to the original baseline and finally touch the last line. That was just one suicide. The suicide had to be done in Coach Waters' time frame or if you failed to touch a line you had to die again by doing the drill over.

The suicide drill was usually reserved for punishment when Coach Waters was upset with our efforts during practice or games. If, my memory serves me correctly, I believed that I had to run about ten suicides at the beginning of practice while the team watched.

Another part of Coach's philosophy to make us mentally tough, was to punish you while others watched. Once we won a home game by about 15 points, but Coach didn't like our efforts during the game.

After the final second went off of the clock and the horn sounded, with a gym still packed with hundreds of home fans, and my girlfriend waiting for me after the game on a Friday night, Coach made the whole team go to the baseline and starting running suicides, still in our game uniform. He didn't even wait for the crowds to leave the stands. Many of our family, friends, fans, and even my girlfriend witnessed Coach at his best.

I can remember it like it was yesterday. Coach Waters with a frown on his face, anger in his eyes, and screaming, had the basketball manager put more time on the clock. We ran for about 30 minutes before he allowed us to leave the gym. I was mad at coach that night. However, I didn't dare say a thing to him and I just tuned his words out and ran like everyone else.

Over the next two years, Coach Waters and I continued to have our ups and downs. On a few occasions he kicked me out of the gym during practice and benched me during games. I believed that though we didn't always like each other those first couple of years, we had one thing in common that superseded our mutual uneasiness with each other. Winning!

One thing that I knew for certain was that Coach Waters was a winner and I wanted to win! Years later, while interviewing Coach for this book and the companion DVD, he described me as a belligerent player during my high school years. Webster's Dictionary defines belligerent as inclined to or exhibiting assertiveness, hostility, or combativeness. At 17 years old, I would have worn "belligerent" across my chest as a badge of honor! During those same years, I described him as "Crazy Jerry."

Belligerent Odell (player) and Crazy Jerry (coach), find themselves handcuffed in a codependent relationship that cemented around their mutual, deep internal desire to win, and win big! We both somehow put our differences aside long enough to win basketball games. I was a starter on that year's team, and we ended up winning the 4-A State Championship.

Over time, winning produced seeds of mutual respect that germinated into fertile soil of success. The following summer, Coach wanted the whole team to attend Clemson University's basketball camp. To raise money for the cost of the camp, someone came up with the idea that we would sell a cleaning kit consisting of sponges.

We were made to put on our Middleton High School Basketball warm up tops and go door-to-door in the Orange Grove community and solicit orders for our fundraiser. To my surprise, going door-to-door to strangers, asking them to support Middleton Basketball, was one of the more enjoyable entrepreneurial experiences of my young life. We raised a ton of money and I am sure that the people who ordered those sponges, only did so because of the name across our warm up jackets read: Middleton Razorbacks.

After a week at Clemson University's basketball camp, Jerry took Tommy Grant and I to Milledgeville, Georgia to attend another basketball camp named B C All-Stars. B C All-Stars was an "invitation only" camp that was designed for the best 150 high school basketball players in the country. Tommy Grant, our starting center had received an invitation, and somehow, Jerry worked it out so that I could attend too. While attending B C All- Stars camp, I was exposed to many of the top coaches and competed against many of the top players in the country. *What an eye opening experience!*

The following year, the excitement around Middleton basketball was ever–present.

However, since we were the defending state champions, Jerry was on overdrive. Jerry always wanted to award those who were the toughest, meanest, and smartest players during practice. Jerry believed in players, especially his leaders and starters, must go all out every second of practice, in every drill! Remember, I was not a practice player. I was a "gamer," one who would always come through in the big games. I believed in practicing hard when I felt like practicing hard or during my favorite drills. However, when the "lights went on" and it was game time, my performance and leadership were always at the top of the team. That was not good enough for Coach, he demanded maximum effort from everyone all of the time. Jerry had a few "toughening you up" drills that he did from time-to-time that I really enjoyed. He would divide the team in half and send one half to one end of the court and the other half to the other end of the court. He would then stand at half court and slowly roll the basketball towards the midcourt circle. The same time, two players, one from each end of the basketball court would race to the ball and dive on the floor to gain possession of the basketball. Many times, players would either get bruised, or on rare occasions, bloodied-up during these drills. I loved them because it showed just how much heart and courage that each player possessed. I also liked this drill, because it always pleased

Jerry to have us go against each other. Practicing hard was always the big "rub" between Coach Jerry Waters and me. He demanded that it was always going to be his way and I believed that it would be his way part of the time and my way the other part.

That year we lost to Orangeburg Wilkerson in the state championship game played at Francis Marion College. Many of our starters didn't have a good game at all. I scored 36 points and grabbed 18 rebounds in the loss.

I remember many of my teammates crying after the game in the lock room. After listening to Jerry's postgame speech, I concluded that I had given it my best shot and proved to Jerry that I was still a "gamer." So without shedding a tear, which at that time I viewed as a sign of weakness, I kindly took a shower and headed to the team bus. Little did we know that Coach Jerry Waters would be leaving Middleton High in the coming months to be the head basketball coach at the University of the South, often referred to as Sewanee. Jeff Runge, who is now a medical doctor, living in Chapel Hill, North Carolina, was the student body president at Middleton High while Jerry was coaching.

When he went to Sewanee and discovered that they needed a coach, he told the headmaster about his old high school coach, Jerry Waters. The University contacted Coach Waters and coach jumped at the chance to move up into the ranks of coaching on the college level.

Coach Waters affected and influenced so many people. Here are some words from a few former players who agreed to share a few thoughts about Coach Waters during the Middleton years:

Arthur Anastopoulo (Director of Tennis, Portofino Island)

I will always treasure the opportunity to be a part of Coach Waters' system, and to be a part of two South Carolina State Champion basketball teams and a 54 game winning streak. Coach Waters never made a big deal about our Championships or winning streaks, all he asked of us was that we do the best that we could, in practice, games, and off the court. Coach Waters gave me the opportunity to learn what disciple; hard work was about, and instilled confidence in me to know that I could be a champion as an individual, and as a team member.

Coach Waters invested in many people's lives. I can say without a doubt that Coach Waters made me the person that I am today, and I will always be grateful and thankful for that.

Frank Russ (Retired Business Executive)

I played high school basketball for Coach Jerry Waters from 1976-1978. During that time I had many experiences that would mold me into the man I would later become.

I was a 5'9" point guard for a team that won many games as well as a state championship with Coach Waters. He taught me the role of this position. I was not a scorer but rather a distributor of the ball so as to make it easier for all of the athletes I was surrounded by to score. He instilled in me how important this role was to the success of this team. I was not a rebounder either but all defensive rebounds were given to me to facilitate the offense. In my role Coach had motivated me to have the necessary skill set to excel at this position. Be the best ball handler, the best passers, best free throw shooter, know the offense and know your personnel as well as your competition.

My point is that Coach Waters taught me how important one person's role can contribute to the overall success of a team. The strength of five players knowing their roles and playing together was much stronger than the individuals.

With this being said it took more to play at Coach Waters' high expectations. I learned what it really meant to "work hard". I also learned what it meant to be a tough competitor. Our practices were physically demanding on all of us. Sometimes our scrimmages were more competitive than our games. Coach would set the bar of competition much higher in practice so that we were not overwhelmed by any of our games. I can honestly say I never walked on the court for a high school game where I didn't think we were going to win. With preparation Coach instilled a high confidence in all of us.

Through Coach Waters I witnessed what it meant to be passionate about something. He demanded a lot from his players and in return we would experience success although some may think of it as over the top work effort. But that's what it is all about.

We had outworked many teams before we ever took the court. I can remember an away game loss where the defeat came by poor free throw shooting. When we got back to our home gym that night Coach decided we would stay at the gym for a while until everyone shot 100 free throws.

These lasting impressions I received from Coach during my teenage years set a foundation for my character as I went on to play baseball in college and have a business career during my adult life. At 52 I am happy to have Jerry Waters as my friend and even more grateful to have had him as a Coach and a mentor. Hard work, being passionate about something, setting high goals, being competitive and working well with others are still great attributes to have in order to be successful in life.
Thanks Coach!

Vincent Porcher (formerly Gilchrist) MHS Class of 1978

Here are many comments about Coach Waters for you, from my point of view: As a male student/athlete in the 70s, it was very important to have an environment that is positive and supportive.

This is what I found at Middleton High School and the creator of this environment was Coach Waters. He came to this new school in Charleston and quickly established the basketball program and an environment of success that is based on hard work, teamwork, communication and sacrifice. There were students/athletes who were better than some of the players on the team but were not willing to do things the "Razorbacks" way and they were not members of the team.

These lessons, I still use today, with my family and within my profession. But, as a product of a single-mother family, the environment at Middleton High School was instrumental to my development as a man and one of the creators of that environment was Coach Waters. I never once recalled a moment in my time at MHS of being poor, being a minority, being anything other than a winner and a member of something special!

The relationships that I had at Middleton with many of my former alumni still exist today, because of our time at Middleton High School and the environment that we were in that allo- wed all students, black and white, rich and poor, to study together, to socialize together and to become lifelong friends! Thank you, Coach! All of Razorback Nation, especially those who were at the school during the first eight (8) years, will always be in debt to you!

Clark Westall (Successful Business man)

My first contact with Coach Waters came during my sophomore year at Middleton High School. I was intending to play on JV again; however Coach had different aspirations for me. In fact, I became a starter over more talented players including Odell, and we became a cohesive unit during the 1977-1978 season going on and winning the state championship that year.

Everyone was returning that year so things looked promising however my family moved to Louisiana and I decided to join them also. During mid-season I move back to South Carolina during Christmas by myself and there was an instant problem. Most of the Afro-American players boycotted and decided not to play because of my return.

Coach Waters to his credit did not concede to their demands and we played without them and won easily anyway.

Eventually the players returned, we went back to the state championship but lost to a better team that year. Coach Waters left that year and well as I did the same.

What I remember most about Coach was our many horse games and one on one game during lunch break and he never beat me one on one but horse at times. I became extremely competitive by constantly being pushed by more talented players which made me competitive in life. I remember getting benched for attempting a wide open dunk instead of passing to a wide open Frank Russ which was the last time I tempted that move.

My father was a former coach, but by playing in front of better players caused me to become better and our chemistry was second to none. In my life I play to win and there is no thought of failing in life an attribute of Coach Waters and I believe he helped steer others in life more than he did me but you will always be much appreciated in my lifetime. God bless you Coach.

William (The Hawk) Hawkins

As I recall, and it has been over thirty years, we were going through a stretch of time where "Coach" was very intense. Practices were always intense, but during this time it was a little different. Maybe he knew the type of competition we would be facing in the near future; maybe he didn't believe we were playing to our potential, or maybe he simply just got some sort of sadistic pleasure watching us tear and claw at each other for hours on end (just kidding); but at any rate we were going through a stretch of the most brutal practices I can ever recall. It felt to me like he was a commander preparing soldiers for a tremendous battle in which he knew that probably none of us would survive. No mercy, no quarter, no prisoners.

Our practices during this time truly were beyond description. I truly believe that we had less competitive games than we did most of our practices. I long wondered why we didn't charge admission and make a gate everyday for them. Coach had no favourites; he was just mean as hell to everyone. I didn't want to let the Coach's down. I had worked hard and earned a bit more playing time and a lot more respect from them.

Through this, life has taught me some lessons that I don't even question anymore. Aside from not pulling on Superman's cape, or spitting into the wind, I have learned that as in the parable about the bird the cow and the cat, that "not everyone who gives you crap is your enemy" (you'll have to read the parable to know what I mean). I learned through this that life sometimes is hard, harsh and unfair but you have to keep playing even when nobody is calling any fouls or even if no one cares, I have learned you have to be true to yourself and follow your heart, sometimes the difference between right and wrong can be found within yourself. I've found that being a part of something greater than your self can be the most rewarding of all gifts. Thanks Coach.

The Middleton Way – David C. Waring (Bobo)

From the inception when the Middleton High School Razorback was formed in 1970 after a decision form the Charleston County School Board to split St. Andrews High into two public high schools in the West Ashley area of Charleston, South Carolina, the Middleton High School mystique began.

During the early seventies when Middleton High School was integrated, this was during the height of racial tensions among blacks and whites, and it was at its peak in the state of South Carolina as well as throughout the South.

Bringing black and white students together from all walks of life that had never interacted nor had they engaged in any social activities alone could have been a time bomb waiting to explode for a new school on the block. With the splitting of St. Andrews High which was an all white high school with half of its student body moving and the black student coming from Wallace High School which was an all black high school the fabric of the two schools were not going to ever be the same again. This was a historical mark that changed all those students' lives forever, being that they were going to be the first integrated class at Middleton High School.

Under the leadership of Mr. John Kicklighter administrator (principal) and his facility and staff buying into his leadership style during this transition, Principal John Kicklighter was then able to work on galvanizing the student body academically making sure that all students received the same quality of education and everyone was treated equally in the class rooms and on campus at Middleton High School.

While Principal John Kicklighter was shoring up the student body, the educational program was making progress. Middleton High experienced a significant phenomenon during this time because the faculty, staff and parents of MHS created a synergy and exhilaration from excellence in Academics, Sports, and the Arts.

Now the ball was in Coach Jerry Waters hands to build a power house basketball athletic program that would bring the student body and the community together to engage everyone athletically and socially with his winning philosophy. With Middleton High being a predominately all white high school at inception, and the majority of the basketball players on the basketball team coming from Wallace High School which was an all black high school with good athletics and had a winning track record.

Coach Waters now needed to gain the players trusts and get them to believe in him and his coaching philosophy in building a power house basketball athletic program. In sports they call it games on, and now it was time for Coach Water to bring it and build it or drop it and flop it for a first year men high school basketball head coach.

In bringing it and building the basketball mystique, Coach Waters' philosophy at Middleton High School was clear from day one. Everyone associated with the basketball program had to have the same goals:

(1) Play hard; (2) Play smart; (3) Play with enthusiasm; (4) Play together that meant unselfishly and execute each play like clockwork. Although the assistance coaches, ball boy and managers did not play in the games, they too had to be on top of their game and run their task as tight as if they were on the floor playing in a championship game.

Through Coach Waters' commitment to his players, faculty, staff and parents' synergy and exhilaration from excellence in sports to bring it and building it, the players bought into the coach's philosophy and his teams won the South Carolina 4-AAAA State Basketball Championship in 1970, 1972, 1974 & 1977 and Lower State Titles in 1973 & 1978. The School achieved numerous Region titles to go alone with the championship in the school's first several years of conception.

During Coach Waters' tenure at Middleton High School which was from 1970-1978, he accrued more than 100 victories, including 54 consecutive wins, a South Carolina 4A record, and a perfect 28-0 season.

Now that you have a feeling for the bench mark of what the Middleton High School basketball program meant to every kid that wanted to play

on the basketball team from West Ashley area and the community, this is where my story begins.

As a young lad, basketball really was not a big part of my life yet, I wanted to be like Evil Knievel and race motorcycles because it was challenging and there were not any blacks that I knew of in the sport at the time. Not that I wanted to be different, but that was all that I knew and had establish my own identity, working on cars and rebuilding motors was what made me the happiest. I would go home with Robbie Walsh who was my child hood friend to work on his father's racing car after work, his father Bob Walsh who owned Custom Speed & Sport where I worked as a shop keeper and mechanic helper. The family took me under their wings and allowed me the opportunity to attend motorcycle and car races.

One day while I was over to Robbie's house, he and I took a break from working on the car and went out to play with some of kid for around the neighborhood. While jumping ramps, barrels, and some of the kids with our bikes. We noticed that there was a new family that just moved into the neighborhood and the kid was shooting hoops in his driveway, so we went over to introduce ourselves and to ask him if we could play with him.

He said yes and we began playing around the world, twenty-one and we eventually played one-on-one to test our skills against his. I was introduced to basketball and enjoyed it. The kid that we were introduced to was named Kevin Jenkins. Kevin was a freshman high school basketball player for Bishop England High School. His father was Coach Jenkins, the coach for James Island High School.

Now that I had gained the confidence and courage to think that I can play basketball, I moved my basketball skill over to Gaines Park; this is where the real "ballers" and the want to be "ballers" played.

I knew most of the guys because we grew up together in the Savage Road and Orleans Gardens area. Most of the real "ballers" were already playing organized sports and had started to develop a reputation as a future Middleton High School basketball player; like Chris Brown, Bobby Taylor, Tony Bolds, and Herb Washington just to name a few. On Gaines Park these were some of the main guys that would be picked in the top five to play in pick-up games on teams with or against present and past Middleton High School basketball players, to me, those guys were real good.

At first, I knew that I did not have the same basketball skills, but I was willing to start working hard on developing my basketball skills so that I could hold my own on the court with them. Once I felt that I could play with these guys, I wanted to prove that I was also one of the potential up and coming players too.

Now that I'm playing every day on Gaines Park with these guys, they introduced me to basketball at a higher level of play, this is when I began to realize the Middleton High School mystique, by hanging around the guys, they taught me what to expect if I wanted to play on the school's basketball team.

Now that I have gained confidence and respect of some of the better players on Gaines Park, I decided to sign up to play on St. Andrews Park youth basketball league to check my basketball skills. This phase of my basketball experience died before it got started. I never got the opportunity to play because the league officials would not let me play any of the teams because I did not make the teams league scheduled meeting so that I can be picked up by one of the league coaches to play on his team.

Fast forwarding to the next basketball season, with very little experience playing organized basketball under my belt, I decided to try out for the Middleton High School JV Basketball team. Now I'm at the ground floor of trying to make the basketball team against every eight graders and freshmen basketball players from Wallace Middle, C.E Williams Middle and Middleton High Schools. The competition was stiff and those guys that were projected to play for Middleton High School basketball program already had a spot on the team and there were only about four slots opened for the rest of thirty or so players hoping to make the team.

I happened to be one of those thirty or so players hoping to make the JV basketball team.

I don't know if I was the eleventh or twelfth player picked, but now I too can experience the Middleton High School mystique.

Coach Atkinson's philosophy and goals was the same as Coach Waters: (1) Play hard; (2) Play smart; (3) Play with enthusiasm; (4) Play together that meant unselfishly and execute each play like clockwork. During my JV basketball playing years the teams I played on went 25 and 1 with a perfect 13-0 season and was part of the Varsity team that won the state championship in 1977. And during my Varsity playing years the winning way continued, we went to the lower two consecutive years but lost in the lower state championship games.

I want to first and foremost thank Coach Jerry Waters, Coach Atkinson and Mr. John Kicklighter for paving the way and breaking ground with their philosophies and winning way and building character in the athletics and student body at Middleton High School.
I know that it was hard and difficult for those guys during the 70's because the way the people in Charleston, South Carolina and the South were during that time and in some instances still are today in the 21st century.
I personally have benefited from the discipline and hard work that was instilled in me by attending Middleton High School.

S.A. Feldman (Business Owner)

In the past ten years you have touched the lives of many people in Charleston and have likewise made a great many friendships. Not only have you been a true friend to my family and me but you have more importantly also been a source of inspiration. I say more importantly because through you the word "winner" takes life as an example for others. Rather than say good luck to you, I wish you the opportunity to fulfill the very high goals I'm sure you have set for yourself. Coach Waters you are a truly remarkable man and a "winner" in every sense of the word. Sincere regards.

ST. ANDREW'S PARISH SCHOOLS
DISTRICT NO. 10, CHARLESTON COUNTY
BOX 3098 ST. ANDREW'S BRANCH
Charleston, South Carolina 29407
C. E. WILLIAMS, Supt.

TELEPHONES 766-1921 — 766-6457

BOARD OF TRUSTEES
JOHN O. ADAMS, JR., Chm.
HENRY M. ANDERSON, Sec.
GEORGE W. SEIGNIOUS, III

April 16, 1973

Mr. Jerry Waters, Coach
Middleton High School
1776 Wm. Kennerty Drive
Charleston, South Carolina 29407

Dear Mr. Waters:

We, the members of The Board of Trustees of St. Andrew's Constituent School District, congratulate you, Coach Leonard and the members of your outstanding Boy's Basketball Team. With originality, vision, courage, diligence and demand for excellence, your teams have become a legend in South Carolina Athletic circles. You have brought great honor to Middleton High School and to St. Andrew's School District.

May you and your teams continue to be successful and bring even more honor to Middleton High School.

Chairman

Secretary

Third Member

Prep All-America **BASKETBALL**

COACH & ATHLETE 200 South Hull Street, Montgomery, Alabama 36104

May 24, 1974

Coach Jerry Waters
Middleton High School
Charleston, SC

Dear Coach Waters:

The editors of COACH & ATHLETE magazine are pleased to inform you that
William Graham has been named an All-American as a member of the Prep Basketball
100 Squad for the 1973-74 season.

Our congratulations to you both on receiving this important national
recognition! The Prep All-America honor is a tribute to your athlete's
superior athletic skills as well as to your coaching ability.

On behalf of the Selection Committee, I am enclosing an official Award
Certificate commemorating William's selection to the 100 Squad. It is our
suggestion that, as his coach, you sign the certificate for your school and
arrange a formal presentation at a later date. And in recognition of his
achievement, your athlete will be featured in the introductory pages of the
1973-74 PREP ALL-AMERICA BASKETBALL Yearbook.

Also enclosed, please find your complimentary copy of the May/June issue
of COACH & ATHLETE. This edition contains the first official announcement of
the Prep 100 Squad, Super Ten Team and Cum Laude winners.

Please accept our sincere thanks for participating in the 1973-74 Prep
All-America Basketball Honor Roll and for helping to honor this exceptional
high school athlete.

Sincerely,

Dwight Keith
Chairman

DK:pal

P.S. A news release announcing your athlete's selection is being distributed
to the press in your community. Local sports editors may contact you for
additional information on your athlete's basketball record. Thank you.

SELECTION COMMITTEE: DWIGHT KEITH, Chairman, Editor, *Coach & Athlete* ● JOSEPH VANCISIN, *Yale University*, President, National Assn. of Basketball Coaches ● ROBERT POLK, *St. Louis University*, First Vice President, National Assn. of Basketball Coaches ● WILLIAM E. FOSTER, *University of Utah*, Second Vice President, National Assn. of Basketball Coaches ● WILLIAM L. WALL, *MacMurray College*, Executive Secretary, National Assn. of Basketball Coaches ● JERRY RADDING, *Springfield Union*, President, Basketball Writers Assn. of America ● EDWARD CHAY, *Cleveland Plain Dealer*, First Vice President, Basketball Writers Assn. of America ● ADMIRAL TOM HAMILTON, Retired USN, Past Commissioner, Pacific Eight Conference ● TOM MONAHAN, President, National High School Athletic Coaches Assn. ● DAN FUKUSHIMA, National Basketball Chairman, National High School Athletic Coaches Assn. ● BUD WILKINSON, Sports Analyst, ABC Sports ● GEORGE RAVELING, Head Basketball Coach, *Washington State University*.

Chris White and Hogs capture 6-AAAA crown

After completing regular play with eighteen wins and sixteen of them consecutively, Middleton ventured to the 6-AAAA tournament in Summerville. In the Hogs' first battle, they clashed with the Roberts' gers and mutilated them 72-50. The red-up Tigers led the entire first quarter till William Graham set the Razorbacks lead on a last second tip-in. The Hogs added basket after basket from that point and entirely controlled the game. Freshman William Graham piloted the Hogs to victory by contributing twenty-

The Razorbacks' next opponent was a tough Beaufort team; however, the Hogs managed to come away with a 58-44 win. Once again William Graham asserted his

ability by pouring in nineteen points in Middleton's favor.

In the final game for the Region 6-AAAA title, hundreds of awe-stricken Greenwave fans saw sophomore Chris White and the Razorbacks exhibit their perfectness in basketball to Summerville Coach Dunning and Greenwave star George Cooper. Although the first half gave no indication which team would reap the championship, the Hogs left the court with a 17-15 lead. Middleton returned to the court and wrote quite a different story in the final quarters as White drilled in thirty-five points and Middleton clenched the 6-AAAA championship by a score of 66-55.

Senior standout Randy Chestnut drives the baseline and lays one in for the Hogs.

As teammates Chris White and William Graham stare in awe, Jackson Bennett swings in an undisputed rebound for the Hogs.

Junior playmaker Tommy Moore sneaks around his Gator opponent to score again.

Suspended in space, sophomore star Chris White lays one up for the Razorbacks on a fast break against Burke.

and Row, managers Edward Hymes, Joe Beach, ...Langford, New Team Coach Gary Leonard, As...Hicks, Tommy Moore, Ronnie Chestnut, Jack Bits, Chris Wiles, Eric Hocker, William Graham, ...Rutherford, Jerome Bennett, Senior Batchee, ...Bontecou, Bruce Shall, Larry Meeker, Paul ...ghes, Coach Jerry Warpole.

...defense's big man Larry Rutherford guide another ...bound cost preparing to pass to Tommy Moore in ...a huge struggle with Simmonville.

154

Chapter 2--- Jerry the College Coach and Recruiter

During my senior year of high school, Jerry contacted me again about coming to the University of the South to play basketball for him. We soon learned that my grades were not good enough to be accepted at the University of the South. While I was visiting many district six, four year colleges, like USCS, Newberry, Wofford, Belmont Abbey, and junior colleges, like Anderson Junior College, Coach Waters called my house and asked if I could be on a plane the next day heading to Jacksonville Florida to meet Lake City Community College's Coach, Joe Fields.

Upon landing, we went to Jacksonville University for me to play against other players during multiple pickup games that Coach Fields and Coach Waters watched. After the work-out, we took a two hour drive from Jacksonville University to Lake City Community College (Lake City, Fla.), where I was given a grand tour of the small junior college, then showed their 1,800 seating capacity home court named the Amos Howard Gym, with its beautiful wooden parquet floor.

It reminded me of the Boston Garden's wooden parquet floor. While on the trip, Coach Fields offered me a full athletic basketball scholarship. After a phone call to my mother and grandfather, along with the approval of Coach Waters, I signed the scholarship and flew back to Charleston, SC the next day.

My first year at LCCC we won the Division II championship, were ranked third in the state in the final NJCAA Basketball Coaches' Poll and went as far as the semi-final round of the state tournament. Coach Fields was named NJCAA Division II Coach of the Year, and I was surprised to receive recognition as Most Valuable Player for the 1979-80 season.

By then, Coach Waters had left his position to take the head-coaching job at the University of South Carolina at Spartanburg. During his first year at USCS, he led his 1980-81 Rifles to their first ever 20 win season, a District Six Title, and made an NAIA National Tournament appearance. During the same period, I was named the team captain of the 1980-81 LCCC Timberwolves, we went on to win 22 games that year and I was again named the Most Valuable Player for the team.

My sophomore season at Lake City was one of my most frustrating seasons. We had a very talented team that could have won at least 29 games that year and made a serious run for the state championship. Yet, we finished with a 22-10 basketball season, missing the playoffs. Everyone else labeled it as a successful season. To me, it was an unsuccessful season.

After that season, I really started to fully understand and appreciate the mental toughness and desire to win and win big, formed during my years at Middleton High School. Coach Waters' style of play had rubbed off on me without me really even knowing it. After two years of traveling across the state of Florida, playing basketball at most of their junior colleges, I saw everything from armadillos, orange groves, Disney world, Daytona Beach and Miami's Cuban culture. I was selected to play in the statewide Junior College all-star game.

I was excited to play in the all-star game to get more exposure to all of the major colleges and universities in Florida and the surrounding states. Along with a basketball scholarship offer from USCS, there were a few other four year colleges in Florida that were recruiting me. I had just returned from an official basketball visit to the University of Central Florida. Coach Fields spent many hours trying to convince me to accept the basketball scholarship with Coach Waters at USC-Spartanburg instead of playing in the All Star game.

I called my mother and grandfather and after talking with them, they both agreed that I should come back home and play for Jerry at USCS. A few days later, I returned home and was driven to USCS by my grandfather to sign a grant-in-aide to play basketball at the University of South Carolina at Spartanburg. My grandfather was very pleased, as I signed the papers that would ensure that I would be playing again for Coach Waters. Much like he was in high school, Coach Waters' was still a master at understanding his player's family structure and knowing who held the influence in the family.

I remember Jerry's quote that appeared in an article in the local Lake City newspaper written by local sports reporter Harvey Campbell, "Odell is the kind of young man that is going to make everyone around him better," says Waters.

"He gives 100 percent all of the time. He is a leader in that he does things, instead of just talking about them."

Once arriving at USCS and playing in my first pickup game with the returning team, I was approached by the starting point guard and team captain named James "Woody" Holland. The team captain greeted me by saying, so you played for Jerry in high school? I said yes and smiled to myself, thinking that I have not heard the name Jerry for three years. Because I had played for Coach before, I thought there might be some resentment from the other players. At first I thought there might be a little problem accepting me into the group or that maybe some of the players would think of me as "Waters' boy."

But that was not the case. There was a lot of togetherness on the team. Yes, I was back in my home state playing for a coach and in a system that I was familiar. The most surprising thing that I discovered was the excellent talent level of the players on the team. However, initially they didn't appear to be as tough mentally and physically as a Jerry Waters' team, except for "Woody." I thought to myself that we have a lot of good players on this team and we can win and win big, if we are willing to pay the price.

About two months later, when we officially started practicing, Jerry was wide open with the yelling, running, threatening, challenging players' manhood, and just being his old self. You know to my surprise, I *missed* his style of coaching and was happy to be part of Jerry's team! I moved into the starting lineup in a hurry. The season started and everything seemed to be going well. USC-Spartanburg was ranked number one in NAIA District 6. However, the honeymoon between Jerry and me started warring off around the middle of the season. Even though I was an important part of the team that had won 18 of 23 games to that point, we had slipped in the NAIA rankings to second behind the College of Charleston.

Jerry started demanding more and more from his players during practice. Much like at Middleton, he questioned our toughness, and manhood. After being a part of the starting five for the majority of the games, Jerry took me out of the starting five, as he felt that I was not playing up to par. I disagreed and thought to myself, "here we go again, Jerry's tripping." I was kept out of the starting lineup for the next three games, and when I did get a chance to play I played hard and we won all three of the games.

During that same period, practice was getting more intense as Jerry continued to turn up the mental and physical heat on the team. One practice that I will never forget was what has come to be known as "Mike Gibson's Day." Jerry started the practice off by gathering everyone in a circle and started yelling about how were not tough enough. Since, I was in his doghouse, not starting, and was known as the tough man on the team, I thought that he was going to get on me again. Then I heard him yell at Mike Gibson, our 6'10" starting center, who preferred shooting jump shots from the foul line than being physical in the paint. Mike was a great teammate and I enjoyed and respected his ability to play above the paint because that allowed me to own the paint on offense. Jerry screamed that we were going to do a few tough man drills. I immediately smiled and thought back to my days at Middleton High. Jerry then called out the names Frankie Bannister, a 6'7", 200 lbs. freshman from Summerville, SC and George Parks, a 6'8", 185 lbs. freshman from Clinton, SC. Frankie and George were both talented players and very good teammates but they were not starters. They very rarely got into the games, Frankie had only played in 3 games all years and George had played in just 4 games. When I say played, I am referring to garbage time, the time toward the end of the game when we were blowing out a team and have a large lead. As starters, which I was not one of at this time, we would usually be on the bench drinking Gatorade, laughing and cheering on Frankie and George along with others during the end of the game.

However, this practice was not a game. Frankie started the drill by physically man handling Mike during the rebound drills, and the more the two rotated guarding Mike, the more intense Jerry became and his words were getting louder and extremely intense as he challenged Mike's manhood, calling him everything that you could imagine. To make things worse, he kept the drill going for what seemed like forever. Mike grew tired as the drill continued and Jerry continued to encourage George and Frankie to step up their physical play against Mike, and they did! By this time, the whole team was either cheering for Mike or cheering for Frankie and George.

As, I look back, the scene reminds me of a mob on a street cheering on a fight between two individuals. To my surprise, Frankie who idolized Mike was "kicking his behind" in the drills. Jerry was all into it, challenging Mike's toughness and continuing barking words of encouragement to Frankie.

Mike, who was a quiet gentle guy by nature, finally got embarrassed and mad and started battling back and we all went wild. After Mike started battling through his physical exhaustion and demonstrated his willingness to get tough, which was Jerry's originally intent, Jerry ended the tough man rebounding drill and called for a water break.

When, the team returned from the break, Jerry went on conducting practice like nothing had ever happened. That was Jerry at his finest! Once he was able to push a player's buttons and get what he felt the team needed from the player, like he did from Mike that day, he moved on. He was a master at that, even though I hated it when I was the player whose buttons was being pushed, I admired then, and even more now, years later, his ability to push the right buttons at the right times. After that practice, Mike Gibson was a different player for the rest of the year, Frankie and George contributed more to our team that year during that one practice than if they had played in all of the games. I later found out that Jerry had met with both Frankie and George before practice that day and told them that he needed for them to physically beat up on Mike that day in practice. Jerry Waters was at his best!

I was practicing as hard as I could and not giving Jerry much attitude, because I was trying to win my starting position back because I believed that we would end up having to play the College of Charleston on their home court in the NAIA District 6 finals. We had already played College of Charleston twice that year, we beat them 67 to 55 on our home court and they beat us 56 to 54 in overtime on their home court.

On Wednesday, March 3, 1982, we walked out of the G. B. Hodge Center our home gymnasium that seated 2,200 and boarded two 15 passenger vans heading to Charleston, SC to play the College of Charleston on their home floor, College Athletic Center, which seated 1,650. It was for the NAIA District 6 finals, with the winners earning a trip to the NAIA national tournament in Kansas City.

The closer we got to Charleston, the more pressure I was starting to feel. I did not know if Jerry was going to start me or not. He didn't talk or look at me and I sure was not going to talk or look at him. However, I knew that we both had a lot riding on this game.

It was a home game for the College of Charleston; however Charleston, SC was our home! Before the game was scheduled to begin, the overflow crowd was everywhere.

I remember having to push our way through the swarm of people as we left the locker room to get to the game floor. The atmosphere was electric; without ever saying a word to me Jerry had just listed my name as a starter on the game board just five minutes earlier. I was excited and relieved that I would be starting in front of my family and friends. I remember the announcer saying; from Charleston, SC a 6'2" forward Odell Cleveland.

Then it hit me, if we don't play the best game of our season, we were going to leave this gym losers. The College of Charleston was on a roll. They had peaked at the perfect time. Their team was very good and their coach John Leopold Kresse was capable of going toe-to-toe with Coach Waters. And to top it all off, I had always been a College of Charleston basketball fan. Years earlier, Coach Jerry Baker, who was an assistant coach for the College of Charleston, had come to Middleton to recruit me.

Coach Baker came and watched our practice, he then came and talked with me during a water break and demonstrated how I could score more points If I would "spread my base" when I posted up down low.

I liked Coach Baker and would have surely considered College of Charleston. Then they had a coaching change and I believe that Coach Kresse did not keep Coach Baker on the staff.

The game started and it was the toughest game that I had ever played in. The lead went back and forth between the two teams. Coach Waters was at the top of his game, and Coach Kresse was equal to the task. Let me take a minute to say that Coach Kresse is one of the classiest coaches that I have ever met. In addition, Stan Conley a former teammate of mine from Lake City Community College was "loaded for bear." Yes, the players on the College of Charleston team were good enough to beat us, especially with a home court advantage and so much on the line.

The game was a slugfest! With under a minute to go in the game, it happened! The score was tied at 52-52 with 20 seconds left in the game. The College of Charleston had possession of the ball and they were running a "spread delay offense." Coach Kresse had put his best ball handlers and foul shooters in the game. Stan Conley threw a casual cross-court pass that was tipped by our team captain James "Woody" Holland. The interception resulted in a Wendell Gibson's game-winning slam-dunk with 14 seconds remaining.

Coach Kresse called a time out, but the damage had already been done! We had just delivered the death blow and everyone knew it. Coach Waters' 50Z defense, along with a great defensive play by our leader ended the battle. The College of Charleston end bounded the ball and took a last second shot that came up short.

I remember looking at my old teammate Stan Conley's face as we joyously cut down the home court nets, thinking to myself, "Better him than me." Remember, it was their home court, but Charleston was my home!

The next day's *News and Courier*, Charleston's local newspaper, sports headline was, **Rifles Deal Death Blow.** It also had two large pictures on the page. The first one was a picture of Stan Conley and Al Eads looking dejected after the game and the words under the picture said. "Cougars Stan Conley and Al Eads reflect Agony of Defeat." The second picture was a picture of me shooting over two defensive players with the overflow crowd in the back ground. The article also quoted Coach Kresse describing the game as, "The most disappointing loss of my life." Coach Waters was also quoted saying, "It was a game of breaks and we got ours in the end."

And just like that the final official game ever played in the old Athletic Center was over.

After that victory, Jerry and I were back on great speaking terms. He was pleased with my play during that tough game, and I was pleased with the fact that he allowed me to be a starter in front of my mother, grandfather, family and friends. We immediately started two a day practices, because Jerry knew what it would take for us to be successful in Kansas City at the National Tournament. About two days before we left for Kansas City, Mr. Bob Anderson sent the whole team downtown to a men's clothing store to get measured for a green blazer, white shirt, dark blue tie, and khaki pants. I remember while we were traveling through the airport, dressed in our green blazers, people asking us if we were a catholic school basketball team.

We arrived in Kansas City with other teams laughing at us in our mandatory dress outfits. We were proud of our green blazers and our seniors were ready for business. We struggled during most of our first game, until our leader James "Woody" Holland looked everyone one in the eyes during a crucial time out and said "no if's." He was saying that we do not want to lose a game and then say, if we would have done this or if we had have done that. Woody was as serious as a heart attack, and we all fell in line. We went on to win six games in five days and bring the national championship trophy home to South Carolina.

Upon returning from the national tournament as champions, we were paraded around Spartanburg and even to the State Capital receiving all kind of accolades and congratulations. All of that was nice, but I could not wait to return home to Charleston where the true street "ballers" who played every day on the outside courts of Orleans Woods, Orange Grove Park, Forest Park, St. Andrews playground, and of course Ashleyville Park, where I first learned how to play basketball. Many of those players never played high school or college ball; however high fives from them for beating the College of Charleston was more meaningful to me than the handshake that I received days earlier from then South Carolina Governor, Dick Riley, along with the many other handshakes from the General Assembly members.

The following year, we had a very good season. However we fell short of returning to the national tournament. Interestingly enough, the College of Charleston went to the National tournament and won the whole thing. Go Cougars!

My playing career was over, but I was still a year and a half away from graduation. I returned to school with the help of financial aid, work-study, and working for UPS from 1:00 AM until 6:30 AM unloading tractors trailers. I was determined that I was not going to leave school without receiving my degree in Business Administration. A year and a half later, I walked across the stage during graduation with my mother in attendance.

Coach Waters went on to lead USCS to NCAA II Tournament appearances in 1991 and 1992 and to Peach Belt Athletic Conference Titles in the first two years of membership in that association. He has served as Interim Athletic Director on three occasions, leading USCS to awards for overall athletic excellence. His basketball teams have won over 80 percent of their home games and made an NCAA II Tournament appearance 1996.

When you ask him about his time at USCS he also talks about coaching his oldest son Jeff, who was a starting point guard for four years and set school records for assists.

When, I interviewed Jeff about his experience of playing for his dad, he stated that "it was a joy, because of the love and respect that the two of us share..." During the interview it was apparent that these two men still share that mutual love.

Coach Waters had multiple effects on so many people. Here are a few former players who have agreed to share some of their thoughts about Coach Waters during the University of South Carolina Upstate (Spartanburg) years:

Mark McKown (Assistant Coach Player Development -- Utah Jazz)

I graduated from USCS (or Upstate depending on who you ask) in 1980, after an abbreviated college playing career. My playing career wasn't particularly stellar; I'm definitely not in the record books, unless they have a category for most injuries over a two-year period. The teams I was associated with over the four seasons leading up to my graduation were mediocre at best.

To steal a phrase from Basketball Hall of Famer Jerry Sloan, we had "just enough talent to get a coach fired, or drive him crazy". I had teammates come and go so fast that I barely got to know some of them. Some struggled making it academically, others didn't seem ready for the discipline required to play college basketball, and some left just because they didn't like it. I played for three different coaches in my first two seasons at Upstate. All three coaches were talented and focused on building the program, and all three helped lay some of the ground work for the success that was to come in just a couple of years after my graduation.

Yet it took the efforts of one special man to do the things necessary to get USC Upstate on the right track, a track that led to the 1982 NAIA National Championship and tons of wins over a 17 year career.

I had just graduated when they brought Jerry Waters to USC Upstate and not certain what I wanted to do after college. Tom Davis, the Athletic Director at the time, told me that if Coach Waters were "OK with it" I could stay on and continue my education while working as a (Graduate) Assistant Basketball Coach. Luckily Coach Waters gave me a chance.

In just a few short weeks after Coach's arrival I knew that I wanted to be a coach. Any doubts that I had about my career, left after spending time around this dynamic man. I figured if I could be half as good a coach I would win much more than I lost.

Jerry Waters is without question extremely knowledgeable about the X's and O's of coaching basketball, but it's his ability to get those around him to maximize their potential that lifts him to the elite levels of the coaching profession. Combine that with a keen eye for talent and you have the ingredients for a championship coach.

I grew up in what some folks may call "a little redneck town." Gaffney, SC was without question a tough rural area with a history of violence. I went to school every day with the understanding that there was a good chance I would be in a fight. When I went to college my childhood experiences left me with the somewhat delusional thought that I could whip anybody's butt if it was a fair fight. Other than a couple of players I had either played with, or coached, (one being the gentleman writing this book) I had little doubt I could at least hold my own. The thought that a guy a head shorter and fifteen years my senior being a challenge didn't cross my mind, until of course I met Coach Waters.

Let me go on record and say the thought of hitting someone I respected as much as I did (and still do) Coach Waters never crossed my mind. But, after playing racquet ball with him a couple of times I realized that not only would he have no qualms about fighting me if it came to it, he wouldn't stop. Coach Waters had the rare ability to continue competing (or fighting if the situation called for it) until the final horn, the last point, or until nobody else is left standing.

Whether it was a racquet ball game, or a championship basketball game, Jerry Waters was in it for the duration. His mind would be working overtime to find the kinks in his opponent's armor, and his intense determination would push him through until he had nothing else left to give.

Jerry Waters defines competitor.

James "Woody" Holland (Western Michigan University Men's Assistant Basketball Coach)

I first met Jerry Waters in the fall of 1980 when he became the head coach at the University of South Carolina Spartanburg. I was a rising junior that year and was surprised at the time with the departure of my previous coach and the late timing of the hiring of the new coach. We had improved each year my first two years and the team felt that we were talented enough to have an even better 1980-81 season. We had no idea that with the hiring of Coach Waters that we had the final and maybe the most important piece of the puzzle.

Coach Waters had an outstanding record as a high school coach in the state of South Carolina. He had won multiple State Championships and was known for his ability to not only coach but to motivate and squeeze every ounce of potential from his teams. To understand and explain this talent as a coach is almost impossible to articulate. This was the eighties, before all the modern technology that is involved in the world of college athletics. There was very little scouting of opponents or watching video to prepare. Coaches had to prepare their teams to handle any situation presented during that forty minute game and also make the necessary adjustments within the game to give their team the best chance to win. Jerry Waters was a MASTER with this part of the game.

Every new coach when taking over a program has to instill an identity that they want their teams to be known for on the court. If you were to talk with any of Coach Waters' former players, I believe they would say, to a man, how **demanding** Coach Waters was with them and the teams they played on. If you were to talk to former opponents of Coach Waters, they would say how **tough** Coach Waters' teams were to play against. I truly believe Coach Waters knew these two traits went hand in hand when he was preparing teams to not only win games but to win Championships.

Jerry Waters demonstrated his championship coaching style right away leading our 1980-81 team to an N.A.I.A. District Six Championship in his first year. He took a somewhat fragile group of guys due to a coaching change, and somehow convinced us to buy into his philosophy in a short five month window. He convinced us that if we worked extremely hard and paid attention to detail that we would have tremendous success.

Many coaches would have been very pleased with the success Coach Waters experienced in his first season and allowed their team to pat themselves on the back and live in the past. Anyone who played or coached with Jerry Waters knows this may be what separates him from his peers. The 1981-82 pre-season may have been one of the most intense pre-seasons I have ever been associated with in my athletic career. Coach Waters pushed our team to a level that most, if not all of us knew we had in us. The results of that pressure truly created a diamond, a team that was able to reach deep within itself and produce a season that should never be forgotten. **"The 1982 NAIA NATIONAL CHAMPIONSHIP."**

Coach Waters went on to have many more outstanding seasons. I am sure that players on those teams will tell stories of how they were motivated and influenced by Coach Waters. I'm just happy and proud that I have been allowed to share mine.

Jerry Waters may not be one of the more recognized names when it comes to big name college coaches but he is truly respected by his peers by what he has accomplished and the way he has handled himself in his career.

James P. Holland -- Point Guard -- 1982 National Championship Team

Clay Price (Educator/ Coach – Atlanta, GA)

I am fortunate to have worked for Coach Jerry Waters for seven years as an assistant basketball coach. When I am asked about Coach Waters there are several things that come to mind and gratitude is the first. He took a chance on a recent college graduate and gave him his first coaching job filled with responsibilities. My brother had played for Coach Waters at The University of the South, so when he was hired at University of South Carolina at Spartanburg I contacted him about a position on his staff. We met, and he said he didn't really have much to offer, but an opportunity. I was willing to learn, and I truly did. I'm eternally grateful for that opportunity.

Coach was, and I'm sure still is a competitor. Returning to the state of South Carolina where he had outstanding success at Middleton High School motivated Coach Waters to show others he could make the transition to college. I quickly learned just how competitive Coach Waters was both on and off the court. He wanted excellence from himself and from those around him. Remember, this was the early 1980's, and he was more demanding of his players than most of today's coaches. I'm sure each player has a story that would express that coaching style; however everyone respected Coach's drive for success.

While at USCS, we were very fortunate to have talented players over the years, and Coach believed that demanding hard work, combined with that talent would lead to championships. This formula worked over the years for Coach Waters' teams and they compiled a 364-133 record. They captured several district and conference championships, notably a NAIA National title in 1982: a memory I'll never forget.

Jerry Waters would not be the name that most would consider when thinking of all-time successful collegiate basketball coaches in the state of South Carolina, but his record speaks for itself. For all of those players and coaches that had the chance to be under his tutelage, he is at the top of the list.

I am still coaching today some 32 years later and I still incorporate with my team several things I learned from him. Like most coaches much of which I know I've stolen from other coaches and Coach Waters is truly high on that list.

Brett Tolliver (Actor – Films, Commercials, Television)

When I was asked by the author to prepare my thoughts on the subject of this book, my mind went back in time. I fondly recall my college days with a lot of pleasant memories and most of them are based on my time spent with the U.S.C.S team. I was Coach Jerry Waters' first mgr and was a part of the U.S.C.S national championship team (82). At the time being a lot younger and not as wise as I am now, I did not realize what a great accomplishment that was. We had shocked the small time college basketball world and became the first team from South Carolina to win a basketball national championship (the same year 65 miles up the road-Clemson won an *N.C.A.A* football national championship).

If you were a fan you would give most of the credit to the outstanding team we had. It was an awesome collection of talent but if you were a part of the team......The real story of how that team truly beat the odds and emerged as the best college basketball team in N.A.I.A. That story would start with a man driven to perfection, a man whose intensity and desire fueled that championship run.

Coach Waters stepped on a campus that was not ready for him and soon turned a team that was not a bad team into a team that competed every year for the district 6 championship.

To work for Coach Waters was both, one of my greatest honors in my life and a experience that helped shape me more than most of my college classes. I learned the true meaning of loyalty, hard work and being a team player. Waters practices were a combination of hell on earth, tent revival and a fast paced basketball classroom. I learned so much from watching him at practice, games and bus rides with the team. I knew he would never be out coached, and any game that he was in was a dogfight for the other team.

I also saw the other side of Coach Waters, the family man who pushed his two sons in there basketball lives (the trainer, assistants coaches and me would play on Sunday nights after the shoot a rounds-with Coach Waters---poor Jeff the coach's son would always be guarded by his dad). I saw Coach Waters as a very sharp witted person (most coaches are great at one liners and wise cracks-Coach Waters was no exceptions).

I also saw a coach who would bust his tail to look out for his players, to instill in them a sense of pride and to make them realize you can't quit and be successful. If you weren't around Coach Waters a lot you never saw the whole of the man. When we played away the crowds were always entertained and our home fans were rabid to help the team because of Coach Waters.

Every great coach has a mythos about them, a quality that makes us forget they are only human. I was lucky I saw the whole Coach Waters and how he impacted my life in a positive manner (I coached for 17 years and used a lot of his strategies).

The last story I want to share is this- My first year as a manager, we went to the national play-offs and we were beaten in the second round. As a small college program our budget was tight and I was stuck rooming with Coach Waters and our assistant coaches. After the loss, we were in the room eating and talking about the game- coach Waters was talking about next year's team and he made the statement "next year we could win it all." I will always remember how great a coach Waters was but also how great a person he was. Every person has flaws but truly great people make you forget they have flaws….and looking back I can't remember a one of Coach Jerry Waters' flaws.

Lee Williams (Financial Services, Business Owner)

My experiences at USCS with Coach Jerry Waters were unforgettable. I was a walk-on, after practicing with the team one afternoon. I was so honored to have been asked afterwards coach said, "I don't have a lot left to offer you, but I would like to give you a shot and have you play for me." I was like a kid in a candy store! I had only played one year of high school basketball and now I'm on a college team in my home town.

I thought I had found a new friend, until practice. OMG! Drill Sergeant Waters, what planet is he from? I hadn't ran this much since I left the hood. I remembered one practice, my legs was cramping as I laid on the court in WW3 pain Coach called for players to drag me off his court to the side. And get this, they kept practicing. Barbarian, I thought.

Coach demanded your best, your all and you had 2 choices if you played for Coach Waters: grow up and get better or die in practice. We grew and won a national championship. Today, I thank God for allowing me to be in the right place at the right time. Because of Coach Waters' "Life Teaching Skills" and the chemistry of the players he assembled on the court, off the court, my business has been recognized as the best in SC and a leader in the USA in our industry. And guess what? They call me "Coach". Thank you, Coach Jerry Waters for the shot. :)

Tim Page ---- Public School Teacher

Coach Waters came to USC-Spartanburg after my sophomore year. Our young team had experienced some successes in district play. Enough to make most of us feel like we had met most expectations. In our first team meeting, Coach Waters made it very clear that he came to Spartanburg to win championships for the university. I remember how competitive and physical our practices were each and every day. Practices were intense including lots of bumping, bruising, and sometimes bleeding that made us a very well-conditioned team. He expected each of us to hustle and "get after it" as we pushed one another to excel and become that team he wanted and envisioned us to be.

As the season progressed and we began to win more and more games, we started buying into what Coach Waters tried to get us to believe. We actually started believing we were one of the best teams in the state. Attendance at our games grew, our gym, the Hodge Center became a "home to defend", and USCS basketball went to another level. Coach Waters saw the athleticism of our players and used a half-court zone trapping defense, we called "50-Z", as a deadly weapon to use against our opponents. Despite our performance throughout that first year under Coach Waters, I'm not sure many observers gave us much of a chance in the District Six tournament. But we believed, because Coach Waters had developed mindset in us from the very beginning of the season.

Winning the district tournament and then heading to Kansas City for the NAIA National Basketball Tournament, validated all the hard work our team put into that season. And despite losing in the second round, it only served to strengthen our resolve, as Coach told us we would return and win it all the following year. And as history records it, we did just that in 1982 as the NAIA Men's Basketball Champions.

Coach Waters is a wonderful teacher of the game as well as a master at getting his players to believe in themselves and reach their potential. We certainly were a testament to that fact. He certainly took basketball at USCS to another level during his time there. Thanks, Coach for the experiences of a lifetime, for believing in us and making us aware of what we could become as a team.

JAMES HOLLAND
Harlem Globetrotter Signee

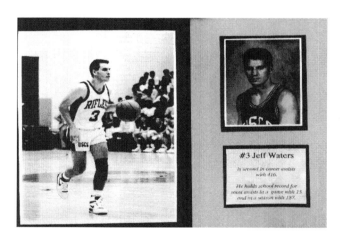

Chapter 3 --- Coach Waters leaving USCS for the University of Georgia

Coach Waters received a phone call from newly named University of Georgia Head Basketball Coach Ron Jirsa concerning Jason, Coach Waters' youngest son. Jason was currently the Georgia men's basketball team manager. Coach Jirsa stated that he was planning on running the same type of program and that Jason has done an excellent job as a student assistant. His plan was to continue to keep him on staff, he then went on to say that Jason was a very good student and represented himself and his family in the best of ways.

Later, in the same conversation, Jirsa mentioned that he had so much preparation to do for an upcoming sixty team summer camp. In addition, South Eastern Conference basketball officials were scheduled to use this camp as a training experience. The officials had also requested that all of the games be filmed so that they could use the film to evaluate their officials' performances. He was concerned about that "camp".

Jirsa then asked Coach Waters, if he had ever considered being an assistant basketball coach at a higher level. Waters stated that he had considered that once or twice over the years. Jirsa then shared with Waters that he had a position open for an on campus assistant and asked Waters to think about joining his staff.

Jirsa went on to share with Waters how he had observed Waters' teams over the years while he was the assistant basketball coach at Gardner Webb and while he was the sports information director at Belmont Abby. He told Coach that he admired how Jerry ran his program. Jirsa started explaining to Jerry what his future responsibilities would be; Waters listened carefully and stated that he had no problem with Jirsa's expectations. Waters then mentioned that there is one small detail that may be a stumbling block if he accepted an offer.

Jerry shared with him that he had twenty eight years in the South Carolina retirement system and that would be hard to walk away from at this point in his life. Jirsa then asked if there was a way that Waters could purchase those two years. Waters said that he had previously inquired and was instructed that he could purchase the remaining two years and what the cost would be. Coach Waters shared the number with Coach Jirsa who then told Waters that he needed to talk with Coach Vince Doolie, Georgia's Athletic Director and would call him back. Coach Waters stated that when he hung up the phone, he was so excited about this chance of a lifetime. However, he wondered to himself, "They might not want me bad enough to take care of the retirement buyout expense."

As noted earlier, Coach Waters was a "Georgia boy" who grew up like most young boys of his time idolizing University of Georgia athletics. He would be able to return to his home state and coach at the University of Georgia, where "everyone" considered it to be "the place to be" in the state. Two hours later, the phone rang and the voice on the other end was Coach Jirsa excited to announce that they had worked out all of the details. He went on to say that he had always been a recruiter, and that he had limited experience at practice organization, calling time outs during the games, and doing individual workout with players. Then Coach Waters jokingly said, "I would not have any problems calling time out and if we need a technical foul, no problem. I have been known to get a couple of them in my career." Both men laughed. Jirsa then requested that Waters drive down to Athens the next morning for a 9:00AM meeting so that they could get things rolling.

The following morning Waters woke early, very excited about the opportunity, and was amazed of how fast things were moving. He arrived around 8:30AM, met Jirsa, who then gave him a tour of the coliseum and offices. The two men then started discussing Waters' future duties, salary and the financial aspects of the camp. Jirsa then informed Waters that all of the other coaches, him included would be on the road recruiting. "And by the way, you only have two weeks to get ready for the camp." Excited about the opportunity of a lifetime, Waters immediately resigned from USCS and headed to University of Georgia. He soon found a townhouse on the golf course, got moved in, and went to work.

His first day on the new job was full of possibilities. He started working on the upcoming basketball camp. Waters stated that his lifeline was the basketball secretary, named Sandy Behr who knew everything about Georgia basketball and most importantly, how to successfully run the summer basketball camps. Sandy had been a part of the program for years, during the Hew Durham, Tubby Smith, and now the Ron Jirsa coaching periods. Waters had already had a relationship with Sandy, after meeting her numerous times over the years, because his son Jason was there and he visited often. Meeting with Sandy and pulling everything together to get the camp going was job number one. They pulled everything together and the participation was great. During the camp was an opportunity to really get to know the players on the team, and to demonstrate his excitement for an opportunity to coach on the big stage.

During this every exciting and busy time, Coach Waters could not help to reflect back on how Jason had become a manager for Georgia's men basketball team. Waters began telling me the story of meeting Coach Mark Salinger years earlier while they both was sitting in the stands at Mauldin High School watching a ninth grader by the name of Kevin Garnet. Salinger, who played for Coach Durham , was now the assistant coach at the University of Georgia and Coach Waters started sharing with him about his young son's dream of attending the University of Georgia and being a part of the men's basketball program. He also shared how Jason had scored amongst the top of his class on the SAT examination. Mark said that he would talk to Coach Durham, and a year later Jason was a manager.

When, I interviewed Jason, he shared with me

the mixed feelings that he felt. There was the excitement about his father joining the program and nervousness about his position as a campus assistant. He believed that his father could coach on this level. However, he had seen quite a few changes among the men's basketball staff during his years at Georgia. He also realized that much like he did years earlier, his dad was presented with a chance of a lifetime. Coaching at the University of Georgia, was a chance worth taking!

Jason stated that he really enjoyed the two years that he and his dad had working closely together. During that period of his life, his desire was to follow in his dad's footsteps and become a basketball coach. He talked with his dad about basketball every chance that he could, in order to get every bit of knowledge that he could pick from his dad's brain.

Everyone who played for or against Coach Waters understood that his coaching philosophy was to play hard physical basketball. That meant switching defenses often and selling the players on the idea that by playing hard defense, the team would be rewarded with defensive steals, which in turn, would lead to fast breaks, dunks, and many scoring opportunities. Coach

Waters never used a whistle during practice, because he always felt that his players always needed to hear his voice. He knew that during critical points in a loud competitive contest, many sounds and voices will be competing for his players' attention. He wanted them trained to recognize his voice among all of the competing sounds and loud voices.

Coach Waters' first team meeting while at Georgia was a cookout at Coach Jirsa's home. It was an informal gathering and it allowed Waters to finally meet some of the guys who were away during the summer. Please note that the NCAA rules would not allow a team practice before October 15. However, a coach could conduct an individual workout session with a player which at times consisted of a passing, catching, and shooting drill. Coach scheduled and conducted individual workouts around the player's class schedule, often at times, meeting at 6:00AM until 7:00AM based on the player's availability.

Waters was also responsible for monitoring the player's academic schedule. He felt that the team was blessed to have a lady by the name of Susan Lahey who worked strictly with the basketball team around their academics. She traveled with the team and at times she would even conduct study halls in the hotel conference rooms. She would always check classes and see if the players attended and to made sure that their grades were acceptable.

When I asked Coach Waters what the biggest difference between coaching at Georgia versus USCS, he said that it was the increased number of staff available to help monitor the players and to make sure that they were in the right place at the right time. He mentioned that Georgia's campus was huge and the players were living all over campus. USCS was a smaller "controlled" environment, and it was easier to monitor the players' behaviors on and off of the court.

During a preseason coaches' retreat, Waters was able to share his assessments and received positive reviews from his fellow coaches. Many of his ideas and suggestions were accepted and discussed thoroughly. He also stated that, "The moment that I realized, I could handle this new challenge was when I first came in and took over the   day-to-day   activity   and   conducting individual workouts. That was my opportunity to really get to know each one of the players individually, because I was the main guy on the staff who stayed in constant contact with the players." He also used that time to build trust with the players. Waters realized the team potential early on by watching and reviewing their practices, scrimmages, and their preseason NIT games. It was very obvious that their strength and conditioning program gave them a huge advantage.

Coach Waters first season at Georgia went well. After getting beat in the SEC tournament their team was selected to participate in the National Invitational Tournament. The team made it all the way to the semi-finals, which was held at the world famous Madison Square Garden, New York City. Coach Waters remembered the feeling that he experienced when he walked in to the old building. The floor squeaked and cracked, however, he could feel the tradition as he walked from the locker room to center court under the bright lights. Even though they did not have many home fans present, there were many knowledgeable basketball fans at the Garden!

The next year got off to a slow start, followed by an up and down season. The season ended with two embarrassing defeats. The first occurred during the SEC tournament in Atlanta. Following Georgia's elimination from the tournament, Waters believed that some of the seniors were not happy about the team not qualifying or being selected to play in the NCAA Tournament, also known as March Madness, or the Big Dance. It was suggested that the team could be invited to participate in the NIT tournament. Waters felt that some of the seniors really didn't want to play in the NIT. However, the decision was made to participate in the NIT. The team selected a tough draw for their opening NIT game, one of Georgia's old rivals, Clemson University. To make thing even worse, they had to play Clemson on Clemson's home court. The game against Clemson was played on a Friday night. Much of what Waters had feared, came true. The team's performance left much to be desired. Georgia lost to their rival by a large margin.

The following Monday morning, Head Coach Ron Jirsa was relieved of his duties and the search for a new head basketball coach for the University of Georgia had begun. As one would imagine, this sudden change in coaching affected everyone involved in the basketball program. During the transition, Waters was granted an interview for the head coaching position, however he was not selected. After multiple interviews, a new coach was selected. Soon after the naming of the new coach, Waters was informed that he would not be a part of the new coach's staff.

Jason Waters at University of
Georgia, Basketball Manager.

Jason Waters at University of
Georgia, Basketball Manager.

Chapter 4 --- Coach Waters returns home to coach Pinewood Christian Academy

After leaving the University of Georgia basketball program, Coach Waters was blessed to be offered a position at McIntosh County Academy. A year later he accepted the head men's basketball coaching job at Pinewood Christian Academy, Bellville, Georgia. This move allowed Coach Waters to be about 15 miles from his hometown of Glennville, Georgia where his elderly mother was critically ill. Once at Pinewood, Coach Waters learned that the girl's team had always been successful. However, two or three years prior to Waters' accepting the coaching position at Pinewood, the boy's teams always had a few good athletes. Pinewood's administration had made a few coaching changes with limited success over the past years. Now enters, Coach Waters, the hometown boy, who comes back home from the University of Georgia's basketball program. Coach Waters inherited a program consisting of some players he had mixed emotions about as to their making the program successful.

Upon arriving at Pinewood during the summer, Waters watched the players during pickup games and soon discovered that there were talented players on the team. As always, Coach Waters worked hard to gain his players' trust and to get everyone on the same page.

Coach Waters designed a style of play that suited his team's athletic abilities and basketball knowledge. He attempted to get everyone involved; especially the few rising seniors that did not get a chance to play much in past years. The following year at Pinewood, the team got many victories that some people doubted they would get pre-season. Many of the players really embraced his style immediately, but it took a little longer for others. The new style was aggressive on defense combined with an attack mode on offense. The team loved the 50 Z trap defense, which created defensive turnovers, which lead to easy scoring opportunities. Waters convinced his team to commit to giving 25 seconds of ultimate effort on every defensive possession. Once the team had possession of the ball on offense, he wanted them to think about attacking the goal. They would then run the set plays that he had designed that would result in either open shooting opportunities, easy baskets, or fouls from defensive players. Waters'

philosophy on offense was simple. He believed in always keeping the basketball and his players moving looking for the best possible opportunities to score. In addition, about a week or so before each team's first game, he would put in last second plays. During my time as a player for Coach Waters, I was always excited about learning these new plays because they allowed us the assurance that we were prepared for any last second game situation. Plays like
the "homerun play", which had a player taking the basketball out on one end of the court and passing it to a designated teammate at the other end in order to score with only a few seconds left on the game clock. I believe that the most famous example of this play was successfully conducted during a regional NCAA basketball game between the University of Kentucky and Duke University. Kentucky scored a basket that gave them a one point lead with about 2 seconds left on the game clock. Duke immediately called a time out and designed what those of us learned while playing for Coach Waters as the *homerun play*.

After the time out, the official handed Grant Hill the basketball, he proceeded to throw a perfect pass to Christian Laettner who caught the ball, took one dribble, and turned and shot it and scored. The place went wild! I remember watching the game at our friend's home with my two young sons. My dear friend was a Kentucky fan and I, a Duke fan. He was jumping up and down celebrating when Kentucky took the lead, and then came the *homerun play*. The very second the ball went through the basket, my two sons and I leaped to our feet yelling at the top of our voices celebrating the victory. My wife, who enjoys basketball also, but also focuses on the feelings of the players and coaches of the losing team. She is really bothered anytime that she sees the players on the losing team crying on the bench or laying on the court dejected after the end of a close game. My comments to her are always the same, that's basketball and she always says "I understand that, however those boys are somebody's son." Years earlier, I explained to her that during championship games, both teams are usually equal in talent and that the games usually boil down to coaching styles, free throws, and last second strategies. One of my favorite basketball sayings is that "free throws win and lose championships -- always have and always will." Usually during last second time outs, the last words that the defending team hears from their coaches is "do not foul," so the defensive player is always a little hesitant about challenging the offensive player on catching the ball and defending a last second shot. It was apparent what the Kentucky defenders were told that evening, as they stood with their arms raised high in the air making sure that they did not foul the shooter. However they also did not aggressively defend against the shot. Years later, no one ever remembers who came in second, except for the losing team and their fans.

Coach Waters' team had practiced the *homerun play* for three years straight, never having an opportunity to use it. I am sure that many of the players may have thought to themselves, "Why do we continue to run this play at the end of every practice for the last three years?" They soon had the answer to their question. On Saturday, February 26 during the Georgia Independent School Association (GISA) AA 2004-2005 State Championship tournament in Milledgeville, at Georgia College and State University. Waters' team found themselves trailing the Warriors of LaGrange Academy by a score of 52 -53 after a successful three point shot that was made by LaDarius Gilbert.

The Warriors faithfully stormed the floor, celebrating, believing that they had won the state title. However, Coach Waters had called a timeout as the ball went through the net, with 1.4 seconds remaining on the game clock. After the officials cleared the floor and they explained to the opposing coach Matt Dalrymple that a timeout was called with 1.4 seconds on the clock. When I asked Coach Waters during one of our many conversations what did he say to his players after they had navigated their way through the Warriors faithful storming the coliseum floor? Coach Waters said that he calmly told his players not to worry because they have been preparing for this situation many times during practice.

He then went on to diagram the *home run play*. I laughed, when Coach Waters stated that he calmly said to his players. I had been one of his players for four years and I have personally experience many times when we came over to the bench down by one or two points with only seconds remaining on the clock. The Coach Waters that I remember, always greeted us with a loud "pay attention, this is what we are going to do!" Maybe coach has calmed down over the years. However I do not believe so. Coach Waters instructed Jeb and Speer to switch spots.

He then told Daniel Lynn, who was the end bounder to make sure that he got as deep from the baseline as he could and if he needed to run to clear space, he could do that in this out of bounds because it came after a basket. Daniel was to pass the ball the length of the court to teammate Jeb Brannen. Coach Waters' last words to his players as they left the bench were that we are going to win this game. He told Daniel to make a good pass and reminded Jeb to be aggressive catching the ball, and get off a good shot. I am sure, much like the Kentucky coaching staff, that the LaGrange Academy coaching staff told their players not to foul. Both teams returned to the court and the official handed Daniel the ball. He made a perfect pass to Jeb, who caught the ball in midair, turned and adjusted his shot and scored a "bank shot" off of the backboard as the final buzzer sounded. The Patriot's faithful stormed the floor and celebrated a 54-53 victory over the Warriors for the state championship. Two weeks later, Coach Waters received a letter from LaGrange Academy's basketball coach Matt Dalrymple.

The letter reads as follows:

Coach Waters & Pinewood players,

Congratulations on an exciting game and a state championship. I really had a hard time with losing the game like we did. But at least I know we lost to a group of great kids and an excellent coaching staff. You guys had a terrific season, but I am more proud of how your guys always show good sportsmanship. Your guys are always respectful and you can tell that they love the game of basketball. That is a direct correlation to their coach! Again congratulations on a great season. Good luck next year.

In hoops,
Coach Matt Dalrymple

Coach Waters went on to say that once he read that letter, he felt that Coach Dalrymple was one of the classiest persons that he had ever coached against. Years later many Patriots basketball fans still talk about that game and Jeb's miraculous shot as part of Pinewood basketball history. As the boys grow into men, Coach Waters said that many of those kids have remained, to this day, as some of his best friends.

Here are a few former players who have agreed to share a few thoughts about Coach Waters during the Pinewood Christian Academy years:

Jon R. Dorminey (Headmaster-- Robert Toombs Christian Academy)

I can sum up Jerry Waters as a coach and a man in one statement: Throughout his career, Coach Waters have been consistently committed to excellence.

I had the good fortune to play and coach in the High School and Collegiate level, and can honestly say he was the most consistent coach I have ever had the pleasure to work with. Many players and Coaches, including me, can testify that when playing for Coach Waters there was no such thing as a casual practice, a lack luster drill session, or a relaxed scrimmage. He demanded the same effort and intensity, from beginning to end, in both practices and games, and he never settled for less than excellence. Everyone knew what to expect from Coach Waters- a hardnosed style of coaching that pushed for perfection and discipline. He expected his players to perform with

intelligence, skill, heart and all-out effort; he was unwilling to accept anything else. By teaching players to excel during intense practices, he gave his players and unparalleled edge, to perform under pressure, and I believe that for many of his players those lessons carried over into our professional lives.

His toughness earned the respect and affection of all those who knew him, as players, fellow coaches or in some cases both. Coach Waters' style of coaching, unfortunately, is fast becoming a lost art today. I certainly appreciate the opportunity to have worked with him; I am thankful for what he has meant to me and will always treasure his friendship.

Speer Brannen

My name is Speer Brannen and I had the privilege of playing for Coach Jerry Waters for two years. He was one of the main reasons my brothers and I moved to Pinewood Christian Academy. I started at shooting guard for him in high school for the 2003-2004 and 2004-2005 basketball seasons. I then graduated in May of 2005, and with the instructions from Coach Waters, went on to play basketball for Middle Georgia College.

When approached about writing about my experiences with Coach Waters, there are several key memories that come to mind. For instance, the first time I ever met Coach Waters was at a summer basketball team camp when he came to give a speech about intensity. I remember him telling the campers that they needed to play the game with the same intensity as if someone had stolen their girlfriend. He then called a camper out of the crowd and asked him what he would do if he stole his girlfriend. The camper said he would hit Coach Waters. Coach then asked him to demonstrate how he would hit him. The camper, without hitting him, nonchalantly threw a fist at Coach Water's jaw. Coach Water's said, well because if you had stolen my girlfriend I would hit you like this. He then bent down, slapped the floor twice very hard, and then exploded upwards from the floor while grunting very loudly into a powerful uppercut stopping at the campers jaw. I believe if he had hit the camper it would have knocked him out. That was the example he used for intensity, and I realized I would love to have him as my coach.

The following year I moved to Pinewood to finish my high school career under Coach

Waters. While there, I learned more about defense than I ever have. Coach Waters prided himself on defense. We would spend an hour and a half of a two-hour practice on just defense. His favorite drill was shell drill, which would intel the offensive team, sometimes consisting of seven guys, just passing the ball around and cutting and flashing, just so the defensive team could work on their half court man to man team defense. Coach Waters always played man to man defense either half court or full court. Never any gimmick defenses. He did not care if you could score; he cared if you could guard your man. He expected 100 percent all the time on defense never taking a play off. His pride and joy was his 1-3-1 half court trap he called 50z. He loved to trap a dribbler right as he crossed half court in a two-man trap, watch him panic, and turn the ball over. He expected every loose ball to be ours and was furious if we did not get it. If you went for a steal, you better hoped you got it or you were going to get a serious tongue-lashing. Coach never wanted us to gamble on a steal or to get out of position. He always wanted us to make the other team have to work and earn every basket. "No easy buckets", he use to say. I realized when I walked into the locker room before the first game and there were more defensive plays on the board than offensive plays, that I was in for a new style of ball.

Coach Waters was always prepared. He always had a defensive play or an offensive play regardless of what the other team was doing or where the ball was being taken out. He was never surprised or caught off guard. His scouting reports where so detailed on every team we played. He always knew the offenses and defenses they ran, who the best scores where, who the ball handlers where, what hand they used to dribble and shoot, what there favorite move was, and who he wanted to guard them. I cannot remember one game when we were not fully prepared defensively, offensively, and everything in between.

Offensively, Coach Waters had plays against every type of defense. He could always get a man open and get him the ball when and where he wanted it. We practiced plays for every case scenario so we always knew what to do and where the ball was supposed to go. He always wanted to take a high percentage shot, which sometimes made it hard to know when to shoot because everyone had different views on this issue than Coach. He wanted a layup! He hated dribbling. He only wanted you to dribble if you had to get out of trouble. He always wanted to advance the ball up the court by passing, crispy passing. We would start a drill over just on one sloppy pass. Never ever was anybody to turn the ball over! He used to preach, "Fake a pass to make a pass!" This was like the cardinal sin in basketball according to coach. He was like a mastermind though. I used to enjoy sitting with him in his office after school just drawing up plays.

His coaching style was that of dictatorship. He stressed fundamentals and preached team ball. Everyone played his way or you did not play. He did not care who you where or how good you were. He wanted it done his way and it was not up for discussion. I cannot remember him ever compromising on anything. I came to respect this very much. He never tolerated bad attitudes or back talking, which I also respected. Though tough, he was always very consistent in his coaching attitude and techniques and never moody. You always knew what to expect and what was expected. He always coached perfection and we always strived for it as a team. Winning was not an option, it was demanded! I could tell Coach Waters was passionate about our team because when we lost a game it was like he lost the game too. He always took it as personal, which made me want to win for him as much as myself. I knew he cared about the game as much as I did.

He despised showing off. No arm or headbands, bright shoes, or high socks. He wanted everyone to look like a team and play as a team. He never wanted one person to score all the points. He wanted everyone on the floor to be involved and share in scoring, again focusing on the team. I came to realize that he did this because he did not want the team becoming dependent on one person but keeping the team focused as a unit. He always expected everyone to play there hardest regardless of the score or who the other team was. He never let anyone goof off or play down to the competition. He approached every game as if it were the state championship and expected his team to do the same. He always wanted your mind focused on the game. No sitting with girls before home games or on the bus on the way to a game. He once told me jokingly, "Women are like bus stops. Whenever one drops you off, there is always another one coming along to pick you up." He told us if we started dating a girl during basketball season we had to date her to the end of the season. No distractions. It is kind of funny because he told this same thing to my girlfriend in high school when we started dating and she is now my wife. She has not forgotten this either.

Coach demanded that we work hard every practice. We never had a day off. He would tell us that the game was our day off. Coach Waters made me realize that you could always dig deeper even when I thought the team needed a rest. Looking back I see he was right, and some games were won because of our endurance. He never wanted to get out hustled. All of our conditioning was always some type of dribbling or shooting drill always practicing fundamentals. The only time we ran without a ball was for disciplinary action.

In conclusion, Coach Waters had a major impact on my life on and off the court. I learned more than I ever have about the game of basketball while under his coaching. I am still applying some of his coaching techniques to my life today and plan to pass them on to my children, as well as the basketball knowledge I learned from him. I had and still have the upmost honor and respect for Coach Waters. I have stayed in contact with him through the years and have visited him on occasion.

Bryan Dutton

I am very lucky to be one of the many people that coach influenced. One of the best experiences of my life was playing for him and later being able to be an assistant coach for him. Coach is a basketball genius and a great motivator. He is a man that all knew could not be out coached. Not only is he a wonderful basketball coach he is a close friend. To this day coach is the first person i call when anything exciting or important happens in my life.

Ric Roderick

As a basketball coach, Coach Waters was great at every detail of the game. From motivation, practice planning, teaching, and toughness to in-game strategy, play calling, intensity, and winning, he did it all and did it very well. When I think about the definition of a coach and coaching, Jerry Waters is who comes to mind. I have watched, played, and loved basketball all of my life. Some of my greatest memories and accomplishments have come on a basketball floor and most of them were under the guidance and coaching of Coach Waters. From long summer camps to state titles, Coach taught me how to play the game with a fire and discipline that I still carry with me today. The respect and admiration I have for Jerry Waters go a lot further than a basketball court! You were a special person in my life back then and you still are. Thanks for everything Coach.

Randy Roderick

If you walked into the gym where Coach Waters was conducting a practice and observed for only one minute, you would leave thinking this is a man that is consumed with winning and an uncaring task master! Actually you could not be further from the truth! Coach Waters love to win, don't ever get that misunderstood, anyone who has played for him or in my case coached with him will tell you away from the court he is the most caring, loving person you can ever be around! Put him in competition and you see a man obsessed with doing everything right, doing your job, fulfilling your roll on the team, and caring about your success and mostly your team's success! Coach Jerry Waters was born to coach, and what a great coach he was! If you ask me three things that defined coach Waters and basketball his way:

1) Ball Pressure
2) Everyone on the team has a role, whether you are the star of the team or the fifteenth man on the team, do your job and do it to the best of your ability.

3) Advance the ball for a better opportunity to score, "be unselfish."

Daniel Lynn

Coach Waters is the greatest motivator I have ever played for. He has a great basketball mind and a desire to win that rubbed off on everyone around him. He knew what each of his players were capable of doing and pushed us to be the best. He taught us to never give up, even with less than a second left in a game. I will always have a tremendous amount of respect for Jerry Waters as a coach and a person.

Thanks for everything coach.

Jeb Brannen

The first time I met Coach Jerry Waters was the summer of 2002. I was attending a basketball camp at Brewton Parker College and Coach Waters was the introductory guest speaker. I scrambled in the gym earlier that morning not really wanting to sit and listen to a speaker but rather skip straight to the drills and playing. Coach Waters introduced himself and gave a little background about his coaching history. It didn't mean as much to me then as it does now, because I had no clue that I would be playing for him within the next two years.

Coach Waters continued his speech and intensity was the topic he chose to educate us on and boy did he. He asked for a volunteer and some poor boy that had no clue what he was getting himself into stepped down front. He asked the young boy a simple question, "If I took your girlfriend what would you do?" The boy replied," I would probably hit you". Then Coach Waters asked," How would you hit me?" The boy half heartedly took his fist and swung towards Coach Waters' face not intending to make any contact but just show what he would do. Anybody else would have done the same thing. When the boy finished his failed attempt at a knockout punch, Coach Waters, jumped in his face and screamed, "I hope you would have hit me like that! If you took my girlfriend I would hit you like this." At this point, he bent his knees leaned down and slapped the floor twice with a scream and exploded with an upper cut that would have knocked out an UFC fighter. He stopped the blow just inches for the boys face. Nobody there expected this to come from an older man, and it was right then that I knew that Coach Waters was for real.

The word intensity is just not enough to describe the speech he gave that day. He showed in his speech what level of intensity he expected us to play at and that is the level he coached at every day. I played for Jerry Water's for four years at Pinewood Christian Academy. During that time he led us to a record of 103-8 with four Region Championships and two State Championships. Nobody we played was able to match the level of intensity we brought to the court as a team and we owe it all to Coach Waters."

Favorite Quote
'Fake a pass to make a pass.'
Coach Waters loved defense. We had more defense schemes then we did offense plays. He enforced more details and fundamentals then imaginable and never let anything or anyone get away with not following his disciplines. It did not matter if you were Michael Jordan or the water boy, you did what Coach Waters asked you to do or you did not play. He demanded your respect, but more than that he deserved it."

"Championship Concentration" GISA State Basketball 2005

Chapter 5 --- Chapman High School

Earlier this year, when I began working on my last project, a book and companion DVD, entitled "*Come Walk with Me,*" I contacted Coach Waters about doing a taped interview to be possibly used in the DVD. The last two times that I had seen coach was at my fiftieth birthday party that I asked my wife to invite about 150 of my friends and family two years ago. I saw him again at the DLW Entertainment's awards event that was held at the Francis Marion Hotel in Charleston about a year earlier. Coach agreed to the interview. After scheduling a film crew, we decided on a date that we might catch one of his high school games the night before the interview which was scheduled for the following morning. We agreed on Friday, January 27th 2012.

Chapman High was playing Greer High School at Greer. That would be his first game back coaching the team, because unfortunately his sister had been ill and eventually died a few days earlier. I was sad to hear about the loss of Coach's sister. However I was excited about seeing my old coach in action and spending more time with him. I then contact Brett Tolliver, an old friend from my USCS days. Brett was the team manager during those days and always a good guy. He is now an actor, doing quite well. I was proud of him and I wanted to share with him my latest venture – the DVD I produced. I called him to see about his availability to join me and my film crew at the game and dinner afterwards. He agreed, and told me to call him when we arrived in Spartanburg and he would meet us in our hotel lobby. After we gave each other a big hug I asked him if Jerry's team was any good. He said that he didn't know because he really didn't keep up with the team.

We arrived at the gym early and sat behind the Chapman bench during the girls' game. I didn't see Coach Waters at first, but then I noticed him looking into the stands. I figured that he was looking for me, so I stood up and waived. He saw me, smiled and immediately came over and started talking about how important it was for his team to win this game tonight. He mentioned that he would have loved for me to have talked to the team before the game. We agreed that maybe another time because this was his first game back. I told him that I was excited about seeing him and his team in action. Jerry soon left to meet with his team in the locker room before their game. The film crew was on the other side of the gym positioning to get the best footage available of Jerry and his team once the boy's game began. We sat through the first half and decided to leave during half time and go to dinner.

The next morning we met Jerry at Chapman High, to conduct the interview. We started talking while the crew set up and tested the lighting and sound in preparation for the interview. During this time is when coach mentioned that he was aware that I had written another book and that he had always wanted to write a book and asked if I would be willing to help him write his book. Without much thought, I said Coach; I would be honored to help you write your book.

I soon turned the conversation to why he was coaching at Chapman High? He said that after years of success at Pinewood, he needed a change in his life, so he accepted a coaching position at Chapman High school in Inman, SC. The decision to move was a very tough decision for coach Waters. His elderly mother was in and out of the hospital in Claxton, Georgia for about a year. Jerry's sister Sandra really cared for their mother along with Jerry when he was able to come home and help out. Because of her condition, she didn't always recognize Coach Waters and his sister Sandra when they visited her. However, he needed to visit her as often as he could. Coach Waters spent many hours traveling back and forth from Inman, South Carolina to Claxton, Georgia. He would often leave on Friday nights after his basketball games.

During this same time period, Jerry's youngest son, Jason was hospitalized in Macon, Georgia with a brain tumor. They immediately performed the surgery. The biopsy showed that the tumor was the fast growing kind and the doctor informed the family that Jason had about nine months to live, at most. Eventually, Coach Waters, and his older son Jeff, drove home from Macon, asking himself the painful question of how the family would raise Jason's two children after he died. While driving, Coach pulled out his cell phone and called his pastor to share the painful news. Jerry, with his voice starting to break, shared with me that the prayer that his pastor said that day over the phone was the most incredible prayer he ever heard. He thanked the pastor.

After he had arrived at his son Jeff's home, he dropped Jeff off and just started driving.

He had no idea where he was going; he was just driving. When he finally realized what he was doing, he said to himself that he had to turn around. At that time he noticed that he had a message on his phone. The message was from his son Jeff, the message said, "Dad, call me, I have some good news. No, I have some damn good news." When Coach returned Jeff's call he learned that Jason's wife called to share that after they left the surgeon returned to their room crying and very apologetic. Through his tears, he shared with her that they had misdiagnosed Jason's tumor. It was not the fastest growing kind as they had originally thought. He then went on to assure them both that his condition was treatable and that he would be alright. Coach Waters, then looked me in the eyes during the interview and said, "If I ever questioned the power of prayer before, I have never did after that!" Jason started his recovery and rehab and over time he eventually got better. During this same time, Coach Waters' mother's health continued to decline and she eventually died.

When Coach Waters first arrived at Chapman in early June, he called a team meeting. During the meeting he shared his philosophy of teamwork and working hard toward one goal. He shared with the team that he had been at some of the highest levels of coaching and that this team was very capable of winning. He also shared that they were a team and they all would dress alike during practices and games. There would be no facial hair, no black socks, no earrings, and whenever one crossed the lines on to the court, he must run. No walking would be allowed! Several of the players tested these new rules. Over time, two or three of the better players fell by the wayside, because Coach Waters felt that no individual or clique of individual was bigger than the team. He went on to talk about how many games they lost over the past ten years. Then he stated that they were not going to talk about winning or losing, but about how "we were going to be the best that we could be."

As I sat during one of our many conversations I tried to imagine all of Coach Waters' challenges in his personal life, plus the challenge of turning the Chapman program around. I asked him, "Coach Waters, what was the most rewarding part about Chapman?" He said that it was the third year, when they won twenty games and went deep into the rounds of the state play offs. Coach Waters then started talking about his sister Sandra. He said that when she was in the hospital he made about thirty trips from Inman to Augusta in a four month period. He went on to say that the experience of losing his sister got his attention. He thought for the first time in a long time that there was more to life than coaching basketball. He also noted that there were many things that he still wanted to do in life, but hadn't taken the time to do them.

He then asked me what I thought about him retiring.

The whole retiring conversation caught me off guard. I said "I don't know coach. Your sister had just died and maybe you need to take a few more weeks to think about it before you make a decision." After, continuing our conversation I soon realized that he had thought about this decision and he had been thinking about it for quite a while.

The interview went well and we finished ahead of schedule. As the film crew started breaking down the equipment, Coach again started talking about his sister's death and how he was so thankful that I had agreed to help him with his book. I didn't think that much about what I had committed to do at the time. Little did I know what was ahead. Then something amazing happened, his eyes started lighting up as he said clearly that he was going to retire and write the book that he has wanted to write for years.

Then it hit me! "Odell the book. He was betting it all on the book." The book would be the bridge that allowed him to crossover into a smooth future by recapping his past; and I was right smack in the middle of it all!

A few days later, during a phone conversation, Coach informed me that he had shared the news of his retirement with his team and all of the "powers that be" in the school system. Soon after his announcement, Coach was doing interviews on the radio, television, and newspapers. The main question that everyone was asking was, "Why are you retiring and what are you going to do?" True to form, Coach answered the question by talking about his sister's illness and death. Then his voice and eyes would brighten as he started stating that he was writing a book about his coaching career and his life.

I never played for Coach Waters at Chapman. However I witnessed a half a game, so while I played more for Coach Waters than any of his players, I can't truly share much about Coach's experience at Chapman. However, the following words from Greg Wilson seem to fit the kind of characterization I would have liked to make. Greg, thanks for agreeing to share a few thoughts about Coach.

Greg Wilson Assistant Coach – USCS 1994 – 98, Assistant Coach – Chapman High School 2007 – 12

From the first time I heard his name, Coach Waters has been a legendary figure to me. I grew up in Beaufort, as a youth I heard many stories of the great teams he had at Middleton and St. Andrews. When I began coaching at Lander in 1989, I received an up close view of his dominant USC Spartanburg team, and his intense personality. Most evident during that time was his willingness to change the flow of a game by switching defenses and often trying something totally unconventional. During that season we were playing them at home, and led them at halftime by a large margin. He came out in the 2nd half and went to a "triangle and 2" defense. It totally stymied us. We blew the large lead and ended up losing the game. I would see that gambling approach from him many more times over the next 20 years.

Five seasons later, I was able to obtain a position as his Assistant Coach at USCS. It was a dream job for a young coach. From the beginning, we had a very special relationship. Unlike his previous staffs, where he had multiple assistants, during my time there, it was just he and I. He became a boss, mentor, and best friend to me. We ate lunch together almost daily and played a ton of golf in the spring and summer. My confidence as a coach grew tremendously during those years, because he gave me so much responsibility. He allowed me to handle recruiting, scouting, pre-season workouts, scheduling and many other things.

What was so different at USCS, than the other college programs I had worked in, was the discipline. I was amazed at the behavior of the players. There was no talking back, attitudes or egos. The players listened when you spoke and allowed you to coach them. That was so refreshing. It also made me understand that players will do what you allow them to do. We had some solid teams during that time, and averaged 20 wins a year in the three seasons I was with him. I literally cried the day he came in to my office, shut the door (like he always did when he had something serious on his mind) and told me he was leaving to go to the University of Georgia. I knew my life was about to change. Less than a year later, unable to accept the drastic change in the program, I left full-time coaching.

Coach and I remained in close contact. Nine years later he called me up and began telling me about the possibility of him returning to the Spartanburg area. I had worked in sales during that time and owned my own business. But I felt that God was truly leading me in another direction. I had no idea that it was to coach and teach at the high school level, something I had previously thought I would never want to do.

In the spring of 1997, God connected all of the dots. We took over a Boys Basketball program at Chapman High School that the previous four years had won a total of 8 games and during that time had the distinction of losing 30 games in a row. There was no discipline, work-ethic, basketball skills or team concept in the program. It was an impossible job, and it ended up being the most fulfilling five years of my professional career. In year three of the rebuilding project, we won 20 games and made it to the 2nd round of the AAA state playoffs.

I believed that Coach Waters' possesses many great attributes as a teacher and coach that made him so successful during his career. One, he always made his practices much more difficult than the games. Two, he had a great basketball mind and loved to X and O with you (some years we would have in as many as 6 zone offenses, 12 set plays and 8 defenses – if I went on a recruiting trip for a few days, I had no idea what we were running when I came back!). Three, he cared about the players and could connect with them, especially the under-privileged ones. Four, his players always played harder than your players. Fifth, and most important of all, he had a confidence that he was going to win, no matter what. That confidence spread to players, coaches and fans.

I am very proud to have worked for him, and he has been a major influence on me as a coach and a teacher. If you watch our team today you will see Coach Waters in what we run (90Z,75Z,50Z,13, Jacksonville, Circle, Russell, High Post, BC, Name Play, etc.). My hope is that you will also see his intensity and toughness in how we play.

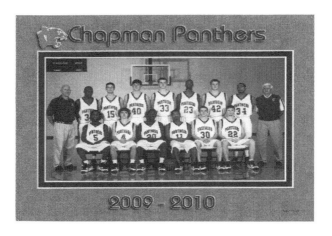

2009-10 (20-7)
Front Row Sitting – Freddie Edwards, Austin Hedrick, Rayshawn Rice, Bobby Jones, Dayton Ayers and Allen Hicks
Back Row Standing – Coach Greg Wilson, Andre Hines, Dillon Grohs, Dalton Fowler, Ryan Gaddy, Jalen Nesbitt, Justin Burrell, Chris Hines, and Coach Jerry Waters

2010-11 (13-9)
Front Row Sitting – Austin Hedrick, Allen Hicks, Tyshun Samuel, Stephen Golightly, Colton Ayers and Austin Green
Back Row Standing – Coach Greg Wilson, Jamare Lovett, Josh Henderson, Dalton Fowler, Ryan Gaddy, Jalen Nesbitt, DJ Lynch, Dayton Ayers, and Coach Jerry Waters

2011-12 (9-13)
Front Row Sitting – Branden Goodwin, Tyshun Samuel, CJ Thompson, Shawn McMillian, Colton Ayers, Hezekiah Williams and Talin Bonds
Back Row Standing – Coach Greg Wilson, DJ Lynch, Josh McDonnell, Josh Henderson, Daniel Forrester, Jamare Lovett, and Coach Jerry Waters

On Motion Of

SENATOR GLENN G. REESE

THIS CERTIFICATE IS PRESENTED TO

Coach Jerry Waters

For Your Forty-Service Years of
Outstanding and Dedicated Service
as Coach to the Students of South
Carolina and Georgia and Five
Years as Chapman High School
Basketball Coach

Given this 12th day of April in the year Two
Thousand Twelve

Jeffry Gnett

THE CLERK OF THE SENATE

Chapter 6 --- Next Play --- Coach Waters draws up the "next play" for his life

When Coach Waters first shared with me that he was going to retire, I thought to myself, "retire and do what, play golf all day?" So, after a few days I called him and asked "what will you do next?" He said that he would be out sharing his experiences as a coach with other younger coaches and the book and companion DVD that I was helping him with, is going to be a great help. He went on to say that he still feels that he can be a great asset to the right program that needs an "old guy" as an assistant or head coach on the bench, one who still knows how to win basketball games. I smiled to myself and said a quick prayer that God would bless my old coach and now my new friend, that he would get one more shot at the golden ring. During the months of our communicating, agreeing and disagreeing as it related to the book, I still see the "fire," the sharp mind and willingness to compete and win that that has made Coach Jerry Waters the legend that he is today.

At times during the interviews and/or video tapings, tears would well up in his eyes and his voice would start breaking as he reflected on all of the help that he has received from so many people along the way. He still reserves a special place in his heart for his grandmother Ms. Lonie Kicklighter. He can't control his tears when he reflects on the monthly package that she sent while he was in college, one that consisted of homemade peanut butter cookies, five hard earned dollars, and a hand written note that always said "remember why you are there." I would think that Ms. Kicklighter would be pleased with her Return On Investment, as her grandson has never forgotten why he was there and has made a career out of helping so many other young men and women come to a true understanding of "remembering why they are there."

He still has so much admiration for his cousin and mentor John D. Kicklighter and all that he did he help him become the man and coach that he is today. I personally had the pleasure of meeting Mr. Kicklighter about a year ago during the 1st Annual Pioneers, Legends and Celebrities Community Awards Banquet, present by DLW Entertainment, Inc. which was held at the historic Francis Marion Hotel, Charleston, South Carolina. My best friend David Waring,

President of DLW Enterprise bank rolled the whole event. David, we call him Bobo, approached Coach Waters about his desire to honor him at this upcoming event. As I understand it Coach Waters requested that there was another person who deserved the honor more than he did a person by the name of John D. Kicklighter. When my friend called and requested that I participate in this event, he started sharing with me the history of a man by the name of John D. Kicklighter and the major role that he played in the history of Middleton High School.

Many awards were given out that evening; however the Legend Award was a tribute to our educators, whom dedicated their lives and careers to the youth in our community so that they become future leaders. The Pioneer Award is a tribute to our community activists, whom have gone above and beyond to improve the quality of life in our community. The Trailblazer Award is our most prestigious award. This award is in honor of the Reverend Samuel Waring, a tribute to our community leaders whom paved the way so those in our community can achieve a better quality of life ethically, morally, and spiritually.

As I sat there and listened as Bill Sharpe said the following words "I would like to introduce the Pioneer award recipient JERRY WATERS a graduated from Belmont College with a B.S. Degree in Health and Physical Education and received his Master's Degree from South Carolina State College has enjoyed a rewarding life as a coach and it is my honor, and privilege to present him with the Pioneer Award."

Then Coach Waters introduced the recipient of the Rev. Samuel Waring Community Trailblazer Award to John D. Kicklighter. The two men hugged, took pictures and the event came to a close. Like most things in life, I wish that I would have had a better understanding of all that he had done before I met him. Sometime later I received a Facebook message that John D. Kicklighter was in the hospital and a few days later he had died. During our interviews when Coach would always talk about Mr. Kicklighter, I would not say much just listen, because I could plainly see that he was still in mourning for his friend.

On the few occasions that I asked him about his sister, who had just died a few months ago. He only talked about how his sister had been the person who took him to church. He went to great lengths to explain that his family went to church, however his sister was the main person who always made sure that young Jerry Waters was in church. It appeared to me as I was writing down my notes that he would always be grateful to his sister for getting him involved in church. I could not help but to think back on all of the "non-church" words that were yelled during our practices, but Coach would always lead the team in pray before every game.

I really believe that the death of his sister made Coach Waters really consider his "bucket list" and getting this book written was one of the things at the top of his list. Many of my family, friends, and fellow teammates have asked me why you agreed to assist Coach in writing this book and producing the companion DVD. Then they look at me and smile and asked how hard is it working with Jerry? I only answer by saying that, I don't really know why I agreed to help write his book and produce the companion DVD for Coach Waters at no charge. As a business man, I do not have an answer that even sounds reasonable. When pressed to give an answer, I can only say that Coach Jerry O. Waters asked me to help him do something that was very important to him that he could not do by himself. I think back to my earlier years when Coach Jerry O. Waters helped me do something that was very important to me that I could not do by myself. To answer the second question of how hard was it working with Jerry? I would say that it was very hard; however I do not believe that it was as hard as it was for Coach Waters to work with a young Odell Cleveland.

I hope that you have enjoyed reading, "Jerry O. Waters, BORN TO BE A COACH." I invite you to view the companion DVD that will share more insight on his incredible story. Coach Waters has had a lot of different effects on so many people. Here are a few Coaches and Athletic Directors who have agreed to share a few thoughts about Coach.

John Beilein --- Head Coach – University of Michigan Men's Basketball

I first witnessed Jerry's coaching style in 1991 during a tournament that both our teams was competing, I was the head coach at Division II LeMoyne College and he was head coach at USCS. He had a great player by the name of Ulysses Hackett and he was running a 1-3-1 trapping zone defense that I later learned was refered to as *50Z Half Court Trap* and they won the tournament Championship.

Ten years later when I was the head coach at University of Richmond, after assessing the personel and talent of my players, I needed an equalizer to play against the tougher competition. I personally called Jerry and asked him to share with my staff the fine details of the 1-3-1 trap zone defense. We taught our players and "trapped" our way to a 23- win season, a CAA title and an NCCA tournament appearance.

When I took the head job at University of West Virginia we taught our team the 1-3-1 trap defense and over a few seasons we "trapped" our way to Sweet 16 apparances, Elite Eight appearances, and NIT Championship. In 1987 the three point shot was a part of college basketball, many coaches felt that the 1-3-1 trap was not affective against the 3 point shooter, many abanded the defense. Jerry and I stuck with it and it had proven to have been a difference maker in my career.

Jerry is the type of person that will compete against you and when the competition is over, you admire and respect how he runs his program. He was great at getting his teams ready to play hard and physical while still displaying a great deal of class. His teams played hard, smart and very much with the spirit of the game.

Sylvia R. Hatchell --Head Coach UNC Women's Basketball

When I was just getting started coaching at Francis Marion College(University), I followed, admired, and patterned my coaching style and strategy from several of the great men coaches in the NAIA District VI. Jerry Waters was one of those great NAIA coaches that I followed and admired. Coach Waters's teams were athletic, played extremely hard and exemplified great team work. Coach Waters was extremely cordial and respectful to me as a young, green, inexperienced but eager to learn female coach. I loved how competitive Coach Waters was on the court and how personable he was to me and many others off the court. Coach Waters without a doubt made a tremendous impact on me as a young coach. Thank you Coach Waters for sharing and caring with this then rookie coach. After 38 years as a college coach, I can still visualize Coach Waters on the sideline coaching his heart out. Thanks Coach!

John Leopold Kresse --- Special Assistant to the Athletic Director --- former Head Basketball Coach -- College of Charleston

Some thoughts on coaching against Jerry and other in District 6. We all had some Division 1 players and coaches. It was probably the best and most competitive districts in the country.The district 6 championship was a game of the giants in all of college basketball, USCS with Holland, and the Gibson boys and Cleveland were just too much for the College of Charleston that night. The following year   The Johnson Center opened in 1982 and it was fitting to have a sellout to have USCS as our opponent. We than went on to win the national championship in Kansas City that same year. Coach Jerry Waters is one of the finest coaches I went against in my 38 years of coaching. He was so knowledgeable, prepared, tactical, and intense. His 1-3-1 half court trap was so effective and a nightmare to coach against.

Gene DeFilippo (Former Athletic Director at USC Spartanburg, Villanova and Boston College)

I had the privilege of working with Jerry Waters when he was the Head Basketball Coach at the University of South Carolina at Spartanburg. What makes Jerry special is that he is a great teacher of the game and his teams were always fundamentally sound. Jerry had a knack for getting the most out of every player on his roster!!! In addition to being a great teacher, Jerry was a master motivator and despite the opponent his teams were always ready to play! He constantly preached that his players are tough both mentally and physically and his teams always played just the way he coached them.

Alan Leforce – Head Coach Coastal Carolina University Women's Basketball

I have known Jerry Waters for many years and his coaching philosophies and principals are second to none. This book will help you develop an understanding of offensive and defensive schemes that you can incorporate into your philosophy.

This press is designed to keep pressure on the ball. The remaining four players who do not have the ball are using retreating-bluffing techniques to slow the advancement of the ball. We contest any and all penetrating passes, but we will allow the ball to be reversed or passed back.

One of our main goals in this press is to cause the opponent to commit a 10-second back-court violation. Once the ball passes the half-court line, our ball-side wing # 3 or # 4 will come up and stop the ball. A double team will now be set with either #2 or possibly #5 positions have two major responsibilities when the ball is in the back-court: 1. When the ball is in their area, they pressure the ball; and 2. When the ball leaves their side , they drop and cover the middle. Once the ball enters the court on #2's side, # 5 drops to the middle and stays. We prefer to have a quicker player on the ball and a bigger player plugging the middle.

(See Companion DVD)

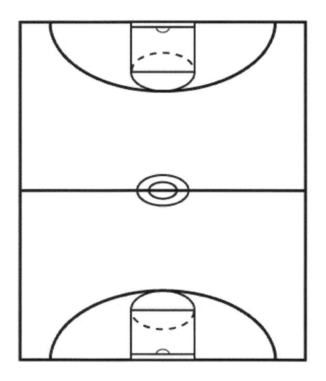

Positions # 3 and # 4 play sidelines when the ball is on their side with bluff and retreat movements. If they are opposite the ball, they cover deep middle and rotate towards the basket as the ball advances toward mid-court. Their stance is such that their back is to the middle if they are ball-side and if they are away from the ball; their back is to the side-line opposite the ball.

This idea has a two-fold purpose: 1. It allows us to re-set our defense again and face an out-of-bounds set that we have prepared for; and 2. It also leaves concern on the opposing team's mind, that the pass was close to being a turn-over. On the next possession the opponent may be reluctant to throw that same pass and this could lead to a 10-second violation.

The first part of this press is really just the beginning and sets the stage for an all-out pressure attack on the ball that is designed to force a turn-over, speed up tempo and make people take a hurried shot with a strong contest man coming at them. These back-court tactics often tend to slow up a fast break team and test their ability to pass and be patient.

The # 1 man starts out as the deepest man to cover any long passes until the in-bounds pass has been completed. When a ball-side is declared the # 1 man favors the side-line on ball-side, but does not deny the side he wants you to throw that pass to so he can be the interceptor. When the ball is reversed, the # 1 must move quickly cross-court to be prepared to intercept any side-line pass on that side. This player must be one of our quickest players with , good anticipation skills. We teach if our interceptors cannot successfully steal the ball, they knock it out of bounds.

(See Companion DVD)

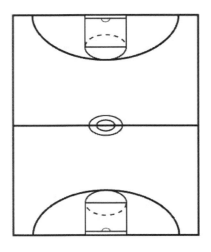

1-3-1 Half Court PRESS DEFENSE

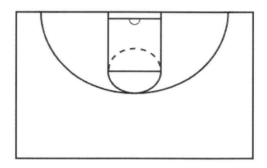

The above position now gets us into our half-court press that can be used as a defense on its own or the completion of our 90Z or Red Press.
(See Companion DVD)

We call this 50Z or half-court trap. This is also a good defense to be used when the ball is our on the side or under our basket we are defending. This defense in the half-court must be played with a very high level of intensity. We sell our players on the idea that if we can go all out for 20 to 25- seconds, we will get a quick score with a steal, force a quick shot or create a violation by the offense. This is a fun defense that players love to play, because they get rewarded at the end with a fast break opportunity. Being in top physical condition to maintain ball pressure for a length of time is a big plus. Teams will rarely keep the ball anywhere near the 20-second time period.

The 35-second shot clock in college complements the 90 Z to 50 Z approach. High school teams can use this as well or they may choose to start at half-court and defend the smaller area. Regardless of how you chose to work these presses, pressure on the ball is the biggest factor that leads to success.

In the next few paragraphs, we will explain each position and the techniques and talents necessary to play the defense efficiently.

THE TOP POSITION- This player must be quick and aggressive, but long arms or good height is a big help. This player hawks the ball with hands up and a stance that directs the ball out of the middle. Forcing lob passes or bounce passes is very important and this player must stay a step ahead of the ball. Any pass that goes from guard to forward on ball-side, then the top men must move quickly to the elbow area of the lane quickly to keep the ball out of the high post. Once the ball is in a corner trap, they can cheat to intercept passes in their area.

This diagram shows the top, wing, baseline and middle men's position on a corner pass.

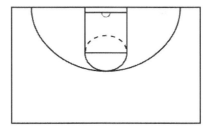

This diagram shows the top men reacting as an interceptor and reading the offensive men being trapped in the corner.

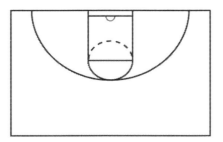

Rebound position on ay shot is to go directly to the opposite elbow and look for long rebounds.

(See Companion DVD)

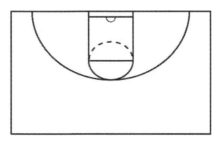

THE MIDDLE MAN- Often this position is played by our center. He must master the technique of playing between the ball and the basket at all times with his hands up and to deflect passes, discourage passes inside, or to force cross-court passes to be lobbed. Anytime the double-team breaks down, he steps up and stops the ball or levels it off as the double-teamers pursue from behind to punch the ball out.

The middle man is very important at keeping the ball out of the lane, so they work hard at fronting players in the high, medium or low post, but at the same time follow the rule of staying between the ball and basket.

This diagram shows normal movements and positioning of our middle man. On quick passes, he must sprint to get between the ball and the basket.

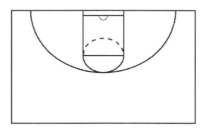

This diagram shows a shot from the corner and the rebound position of our middle man. The middle of the lane is where the middle man goes on shots from any position on the court.

THE WING POSITION – The wings must be very athletic and willing to be hard workers. Their job is simple in its rules, but difficult to play because of the distance they must cover. Pressure on the ball by double-teamers and a middle man with his hands up can force balls to be bounced or lobbed and this helps the wings do their job. The wings rule is if the ball is on their side, they come all the way to the ball with their inside hand up and a stance that will force the dribbler to always go outside away from the basket. If the ball leaves your side you sprint hard to cover the basket.

This diagram shows a guard to guard pass. We can see the off-side wing sprint up to stop the ball and the wing that was in the double-team sprinting to cover the basket.

On passes that go over the wing's head, they drop step and take a quick inside out route to set a second double.

(See Companion DVD)

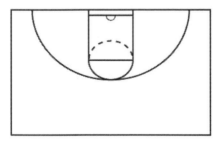

*Rebound position for the wing is the block away from the ball or they contest shots if they are on the ball-side

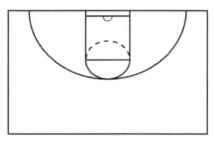

All of this information will, hopefully, help players and coaches to understand the techniques of trapping, bluffing, ad angles people take to be more efficient. Traps are set in the four corners of half-court.

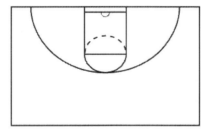

This diagram will show that when the ball is in the wing area, we do not trap. The ball-side wing plays straight up on the ball and the other players play like a
1 – 3 – 1 zone.

(See Companion DVD)

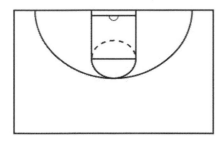

(See Companion DVD)

The idea in this diagram is to put lots of pressure on the ball and if the player dribbles right or left, we move in and trap him.

Whether you choose to use these presses a lot or in special situations, they can give you the winning edge.

Appendix --- 2   SPIN Offense

-1 passes to 2 and gets the ball back; 1 dribbles hard left and looks to pass back to 5 stepping out first, 2 on a skip pass second, 3 fading to the corner third (1 must read the high defender to see if they step out on 5 or not)

-2 gets the ball from 1 and looks into post just as a decoy, then passes the ball back to 1; when 1 dribbles left 2 reads the defender up high – if the defender steps out with 5 – 2 fades immediately, if the defender does not step out 2 does not fade until 5 gets the ball; in either case when 2 gets the ball they look to shoot or pass into the post (low or high)

-3 fades to baseline when 1 dribbles back towards them; 3 shoots or penetrates if they get the ball; if the ball goes to 5 and/or 2 on the opposite side 3 rebounds weakside

-4 dives to ballside block then steps out to short corner on 1's pass to 2; as 1 passes to either 5 or 2 – 4 pins the bottom person of the zone and posts up; if 4 gets the ball they look to score or hit 5 at high post or 1 or 3 weakside

-5 steps down one step below free throw line then cuts across the ballside elbow on 1's pass to 2 asking for the ball; as 1 dribbles back left 5 steps out to the three point line; if 1 passes to 5 they look to pass to 2 fading to the corner or 4 ducking in at the post; if 1 skips to 2 – 5 becomes high post again

This set makes the defense step up and out away from the middle and spreads them out.

SPIN (1/4 High Set)

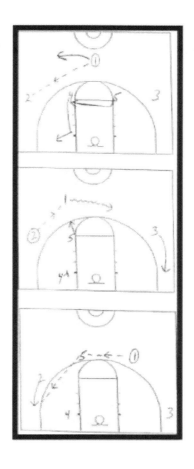

SPIN ¼ Low Set

-1 passes to 3 and gets the ball back to 5 stepping out first, 3 on a skip pass second, 2 fading to the corner third (1 must read the high defender to see if they step out on 5 or not.)

-3 gets the ball from 1 and looks into post just as a decoy, then passes the ball back to 1; when 1 dribbles left 3 reads the defender up high - if the defender steps out with 5 - 3 fades immediately, if the defender does not step out 3 does not fade until 5 gets the ball; in either case when 3 gets the ball they look to shoot or pass into the post (low or high)

-2 fades to baseline when 1 dribbles back towards them; 2 shoots or penetrates if they get the ball; if the ball goes to 5 and/or 3 on the opposite side, 2 rebounds weakside

-4 steps out to short corner on 1's pass to 3; as 1 passes to either 5 or 3 - 4 pins the bottom person of the zone and posts up; if 4 gets the ball they look to score or hit 5 at high post or 1 or 2 weakside

-5 ducks into the rim then cuts hard up to ballside elbow asking for the ball; as 1 dribbles right 5 steps out to the three point line; if 1 passes to 5 they look to pass to 3 fading to the corner or 4 ducking into post up; if 1 skips to 3 in the corner 5 becomes high post again

This set allows the offense to come from behind the defense when making their cuts, which can create more movement by the defense.

SPIN ¼ Low Set

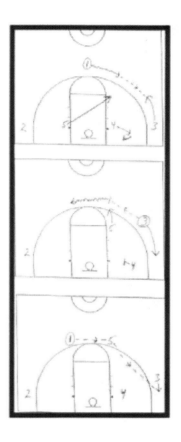

SPIN / 1-3-1 SET

Figure 1:
- 1 passes to 2 at the wing.
- 5 slides to open area at the high post.
- 4 steps to the short corner and faces ball

Figure 2:
- 2 passes back to 1 at the top.
- 1 dribbles away toward 3 hard.
- 3 slides away from 1 keeping a 15 foot passing lane.
- 5 as 1 gets FT lane extended 5 steps out to the top facing basket.

Figure 3:
- 1 reverses ball to 5.
- 5 catches ball as close in as possible and faces basket.
- 4 as 5 faces the basket and catches the ball, 4 pins the backside of the zone.
- 2 slides away from 5 looking fo the pass.
- 5 reads the defense and hits the open man and slides to the open high post area

Figure 4:
- 1 runs to the ball side for the reversal from 2.
- 2 reverses the ball to 1.
- 1 dribbles to opposite side and passes to 3.
- 4 ducks in hard when 1 catches the ball and runs to opposite short corner.
- 5 runs to away side high post as 2 passes to 1.
- 3 receives pass from 1 and dribbles away to run same play to that side.

1-3-1 SET

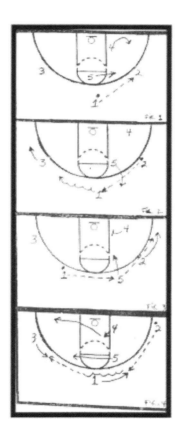

SPIN (Guard Pops Out)

-1 dribbles right looking to hit 2 on the wing, she rotates out a little higher than where she passed it from, then will get the ball back from 2; when she gets the ball back she must change sides of the floor and look hard at the post that is stepping up the lane; she then looks to skip pass it to the corner to 2 on the fade; or rotate to 3 popping out top

-2 gets the ball from 1 and looks at 5 popping to short corner and 3 cutting to the ball side elbow; she then passes back to 1 out top; after the pass she fades to the corner for the three or the dump down to the post (when she gets the skip pass from 1 or the pass from 3)

-3 cuts hard across the free throw line to the ball side elbow; once 1 changes sides of the floor she pops out for the three; or swings the ball to 2 in the corner or bounces it into the 5 posting up

-4 posts up hard as the ball is dribbled towards her (step up the lane in a gap); the she rebounds (let the defender have inside position - the rebound will come off long)

-5 steps to the short corner ball side on the pass to 2 (get as close to out of bounds as possible); on the pass back to 1 from2 screen the defender on the outside, then post up; if the pass goes to 3 and not 2 the screen is off and she posts up in line with the ball; score if you get the post up in line with the ball; score if you get on the post or kick it back out for a three to 2, 1 or 3

*roles are reversed if 1 goes left; this also isolates 4 at the post when 1 changes sides.

SPIN (Guard Pops Out)

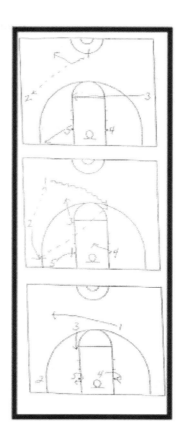

Quick Hitter
¼ High Set

-1 passes to 4 fades to the wing

- 3 fades to the corner

-2 fades to the corner

-4 gets the ball from 1 and faces up in tripple threat position; 4 looks to pass to 2 in the ballside corner, 5 cutting to the ballside block, 1 fading to opposite wing and 3 fading to weakside corner; 4 can also penetrate left and look to kick it out to 3 in the corner or 1 on the wing, or 4 can dump it off to 5

-5 cuts hard down to ballside block and posts up; 5 then posts up in line with the ball where ever it goes and looks to find an open hole in the defense; 5 must keep good spacing in relation to 4

*This is a quick hitter out of the 1/4 high set to get everybody on the baseline and force the defense to flatten out.

Quick Hitter
¼ High Set

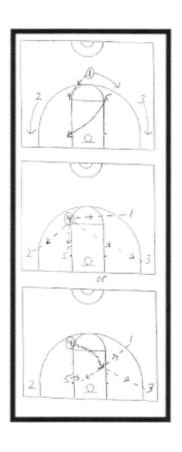

Appendix 3 --- Photo Section --- Memories

Made in the USA
Charleston, SC
27 November 2012